THE WORLD CRISIS AND THE ONLY WAY OUT

Five Unforgettable Messages
By Dr. Jesse Hendley

Flint, Michigan 1956

Compiled By
Biblical Principles, Inc.
Brad Waters & Bill Prince

PUBLISHED *by* PARABLES
Earthly Stories with a Heavenly Meaning

THE WORLD CRISIS AND THE ONLY WAY OUT
Five Unforgettable Messages By Dr. Jesse Hendley

Compiled By Biblical Principles, Inc / Brad Waters & Bill Prince

Copyright © Biblical Principles, Inc
2017

Published By Parables
November, 2017

Unless otherwise specified Scripture quotations are taken from the authorized version of the King James Bible.

ISBN 978-1-945698-38-5
Printed in the United States of America

Readers should be aware that Internet Web sites offered as citations and/or sources for further information may have been changed or disappeared between the time this was written and when it is read.

THE WORLD CRISIS AND THE ONLY WAY OUT

Five Unforgettable Messages
By Dr. Jesse Hendley

Flint, Michigan 1956

Compiled By
Biblical Principles, Inc.
Brad Waters & Bill Prince

PUBLISHED *by* PARABLES
Earthly Stories with a Heavenly Meaning

Free Books for Ministers

As a memorial to Danny Watters a copy of this book may be provided free for ministers by Biblical Principles Inc. through the contact us form on www. biblicalprinciplesinc.org or by other means of distribution. Donations on line can be made on this website. All revenue from this book through royalties and donations are used to make free books for ministers possible.

Acknowledgment

This book acknowledges the financial support and other contributions provided by the following donors which made it possible.

Lighthouse Baptist Church
Port Charlotte, FL

Nexus Financial Group
Loganville, GA

James Lacy, Tree Farmer
Dunwoody, GA

Beasley Forest Products
Hazlehurst, GA

Participating Editors

Felicia Carter
Cheryl Waters
Brice Nelms

Table of Content

Biographical Sketch of Jesse M. Hendley

The "Dean of Southern Baptist Evangelists," Dr. Jesse Murphy Hendley dedicated his life to the proclamation of the gospel message to lost souls.[1] He was born October 11, 1907 in Montgomery, Alabama, to Albert and Helen Hendley, but his family moved to the Atlanta area when he was a child. He received his education from the public schools in Atlanta and later attended Georgia Tech University for one year. Hendley accepted the call to preach and enrolled at Columbia Theological Seminary in Decatur, Georgia. He later attended Southern Baptist Theological Seminary in Louisville, Kentucky.

Jesse Hendley was a natural leader. His first pastorate position was at Liberty Baptist Church in Lilburn, Georgia (now Lilburn First Baptist), from 1932 to 1933. He later served as pastor of Colonial Hills Baptist Church in East Point, Georgia for fourteen years. Under his leadership, the congregation grew from eighty-five on Sunday mornings to 2,300. He also began a radio ministry, in 1931 that developed into The Radio Evangelistic Hour (one of the most sustained and successful gospel radio ministries of the twentieth century). Hendley also served as the editor of The Radio Evangelistic News, a monthly publication that featured sermons from

5

the REH as well as letters from listeners of the show. In addition to holding revival meetings throughout the United States, Dr. Hendley preached messages in Africa, India, Indonesia, the Panama Canal Zone, Singapore, and South America.[2]

---

[1] Bryant, James W. "Sixty-five Years in Evangelism: A Spiritual Biography of Dr. Jesse M. Hendley" – Paper in Jesse M. Hendley Collection, Southern Baptist Historical Library and Archives (SBHLA).

[2] Additional information was obtained with permission from records provided by SBHLA and from their pages on the internet.

Foreword

Jess Hendley's ministry influenced me earlier than I realized. My wife Janet's mother, Velma Denney, came under deep conviction listening to his radio sermons. As a result, she received Christ as her personal Savior. Only heaven will reveal how many he brought to Christ through his radio preaching and teaching alone. Through his preaching, I got a Christian mother-in-law and a Christian wife.

As a very young preacher, I became acquainted with "Bro. Jess." When I was Pastor at West Rome Baptist Church in Rome, Georgia, I had him come for a revival. We started during the Training Session before the evening service. Twelve came to Christ in that gathering! That was the beginning of many times for him to preach in my churches. When I was Pastor at Dauphin Way Baptist Church in Mobile, Alabama, we saw scores come to Christ as he preached. I invited him to preach a series of services at First Baptist Church, Jacksonville, Florida. At the end of the eight-day meeting, 375 had made professions of faith; we baptized 350 of them! It never failed. Always many came to Christ when Bro. Jess was preaching.

Dr. Hendley was one of the most anointed evangelists I have ever known. Though not as well known around the world as Billy Graham, he was a shining light in that generation of great soul winning preachers. His burden was always for souls. I have never known a man to have the kind of passion for winning the lost as did he. This is why he preached with fervor and passion on such subjects as the apostasy, the Great White Throne Judgment, eternity, heaven and hell. He not only preached these truths. He deeply believed them.

Some made fun of Dr. Hendley's fiery preaching on hell. One week when he was with me, we were having lunch together. A local pastor came by our table and declared, "Well, if it isn't 'Hellfire and damnation' Hendley." As the thoughtless preacher walked away, I saw the hurt on Dr. Hendley's face and the tears in his eyes. Then he said, "Jerry, I really believe there is a hell, and I don't want anyone to go there." He implored me to never preach on hell without a tear in my eye and a burden in my heart.

There was more to Dr. Hendley than just his evangelistic zeal. He was a genuine scholar. He embodied the often-heard phrase, "scholarship on fire." He was trained at Georgia Tech and Southern Baptist Theological Seminary. He had the best grasp of the Greek New Testament I ever witnessed. I heard him quote entire chapters from the Greek New Testament! He knew all of the 5,000+ words in the Greek New Testament by their lexical definition. In his Bible teaching sessions, his explanations of them were classic.

I would not do justice to Dr. Hendley and his ministry if I didn't mention his prayer life. Often he would seclude himself in his motel room for long hours to pray for the services at the church where he was preaching. Let me share a story with you. My good friend, Danny Watters, became a kind of caregiver for Dr. Hendley in his latter years. One week, Danny tried to contact Bro. Jess, but was unable to do so. He checked with Dr. Hendley's secretaries at his ministry office. They hadn't heard from him either. So, Danny went to his Condo. He knocked on the door several times, but there was no answer. As he turned to leave, he heard the door open. Turning around he saw Bro. Jess standing there, his face aglow from another world. Denny expressed the concern that he could not be reached. Dr. Hendley said, "Son, I have been with God," turned and closed the door. Does anyone wonder why God used him so powerfully and uses us so poorly?

I could fill many pages with stories from this remarkable man of God. But I must stop. I don't want to keep you from diving in to his remarkable sermons. I am so glad Brothers Bill Prince and Brad Waters have put them into a book. His is a kind of preaching that needs to be read and shared in our day of watered down, weak, anemic pulpit fare. Perhaps God will use these sermons from the heart, lips and pen of this remarkable man to stir preachers and churches to the much-needed revival in these days of apostasy.

Jerry Vines, Pastor Emeritus, First Baptist Church, Jacksonville, Florida; Two-time President, Southern Baptist Convention; President, Jerry Vines Ministries, Inc.

Revival on Moreland Ave., Atlanta

The Sob Of A Lost Soul

Our Father, we thank You again for the privilege of standing as a dying man before dying men, women, boys and girls, with the Gospel of Christ, the Word of God. None of us knows whether we will ever reach the threescore years and ten, Lord. We know that some do, and some few go even to the eighty-mark. But even then, life is very short to prepare for Eternity.

Some of us will never see sixty or fifty. Some of us may never see forty or twenty-five. Some of us may never be grown, of these boys and girls. There are graves of the young in the cemeteries. There are short funeral services held for the very young.

So we pray, Lord, that You will speak to our hearts tonight. Help us to think on eternal issues, eternal things, to lose sight of the things of time and see the values of eternity.

May there not be a single man, woman, boy and girl leave this place until he or she is saved and knows without a shadow of doubt they are in contact with God and that it is well with their soul. We will thank You, our Father, for all that You do for us. We ask in Jesus' Name and for His sake. Amen.

Now tonight I wish to speak to you on the subject, "The Sob of a Lost Soul." I will read to you from Psalm 16:10 and then Psalm 22:1.

Psalm 16

In Psalm 16, David is face to face with death. He says, "I have set the Lord always before me. Because He is at my right hand, I shall not be moved. Therefore, my heart is glad and my glory rejoiceth. My flesh also shall rest in hope. For Thou wilt not abandon my soul to hell."

You will notice that I am changing the translation just a little. The words, "Thou wilt not leave my soul in hell," are literally, "Thou wilt not abandon my soul to hell." The Hebrew words are not "in hell" (that would be buh sheol), but "to hell" (lub sheol). It is, "Thou wilt not abandon my soul TO hell."

"Neither wilt Thou suffer Thine Holy One to see corruption. Thou wilt show me [instead of hell] the path of life. In Thy presence is fullness of joy. At Thy right hand there are pleasures forevermore." These are glorious words for anybody who is dying.

Psalm 22

Then in Psalm 22:1 we have, "My God, my God, why hast Thou forsaken me?"

Contrasted

The reason I have read these two passages is that we have the same Hebrew word in Psalm 16:10 and in Psalm 22:1. The word translated "leave" in 16:10 is the word translated "forsaken" in 22:1. It is the Hebrew word absav, which means "to abandon, to give up, to let go, to have nothing more to do with."

So on the one hand in 16:10 we have the glorious, triumphant cry of a man face to face with death, "God will not abandon my soul to hell, neither will He suffer His Holy One to see corruption," and on the other hand we have the sob of a God-forsaken soul, "My God, my God, why hast Thou forsaken me."

I say to you tonight, if you were dying, if you came down to death's door and could say, "God will not abandon my soul to hell," you should be the happiest person in the world, for you have nothing to fear in death. One of these days you and I are going to leave mother and father and sister and brother and houses and lands and all our earthly possessions and these bodies, and we are going through the portals of death. What a glorious thing to be able to say, "God will not abandon my soul to hell!" Some of you here tonight can say that. I hope all of you can. I hope you have that wonderful confidence that you are saved, you know you are saved, you are certain that God will not abandon your soul to hell.

On the other hand, in Psalm 22:1 we have the sob of a God-forsaken soul, one who has been forsaken of God, one who has been abandoned of God, one who has been given up of God. "My God, my God, why hast Thou forsaken me?"

One is the jubilant cry of the person who knows God is with him forever; the other is the despairing cry of the person given up of God forever.

Here is a wonderful truth and a terrible truth, my friends. God will take care of some of you when you die. Others, He will abandon if you do not trust Christ. Every human being in the world is in one of these two categories.

Exodus 8 – Delay

Now with that background, my text is found in Exodus 8:10 where we read, "And Pharaoh said, Tomorrow. And Moses said, Be it according to thy word." God had spoken to Pharaoh and told him what to do, but he said, "Not today, tomorrow."

Delay ruined Pharaoh. It is ruining some of you. You have been saying, "Tomorrow I am going to receive Jesus and begin the journey to heaven. Tomorrow I am going to get right with God, study the Bible, pray, live a holy life, witness for Jesus, give my tithes and offerings to the Lord. Tomorrow I will be a godly man." But you are no nearer heaven. In fact, you are drifting farther from it because you have refused to get right with God.

"You Must Be Born Again" (John Owen)

During these days I have tried to warn you, friends, that YOU MUST BE BORN AGAIN TO ENTER THE KINGDOM OF GOD.

On the bookshelves in my study are twenty-two volumes by the famous Puritan, John Owen, one of the greatest preachers who has ever lived, a man of tremendous intellect and great spirituality. He tells how he had been preaching for many years when he was suddenly stricken and came to death's door. At that moment, instead of seeing the glory of God, terror gripped his heart! He realized that although he had been preaching the Gospel for years he had NEVER BEEN BORN AGAIN. He cried to God in great agony, and the Lord saved him, and the Lord applied to his heart Psalm 130:4, "There is forgiveness with Thee, that Thou mayest be feared." John Owen, the preacher, was born again as he was brought face to face with death.

God raised him from that sickbed and put him back in the pulpit, and there was a new note in his preaching. He began to say to people, "You say you are saved; do you know it? Do you know you have been born again? Do you know you have had a change of heart toward God? Do you know you are ready to meet the Lord? Or is your religion in mere externalities? Do you know within your heart that you have been born of the Spirit of God and are ready for heaven?"

My friends, that is all that matters. Being right with God is the most important thing in your life. I have tried to tell you in these days, "You must be born again."

No Difference Among the Unsaved

The second thing I have tried faithfully to warn you about from God's Word is that God says there is NO DIFFERENCE AMONG UNSAVED MEN, for ALL have sinned and come short of the glory of God. People tend to pigeonhole people, to categorize and classify them according to position and condition. We classify them according to their business, their social, political and economic positions, and according to race, color, creed, education, worldly possessions and attainments. We have all kinds of pigeon holes; God has only two pigeon holes: the saved and the unsaved. Among the unsaved there are NO DIFFERENCES whatsoever.

You say, "You mean there is no difference between a drunkard in the gutter and a fine businessman, though he is not a Christian?" Not a bit. Both are going to hell.

"You mean there is no difference between a harlot of the street and a fine, upright, honest housewife who has rejected Christ?" No difference at all. Both are going to hell.

Egypt

There was no difference in the days of Egypt. God said, "This night the destroying angel is going through the land," and He told His people, "Take a lamb and cut its throat and catch the blood in a basin. Take a hyssop sprig and sprinkle the blood on the outside of the doorposts of your houses. WHEN I SEE THE BLOOD, I WILL PASS OVER YOU." At midnight the destroying angel went through the land, and there arose a great cry in Egypt because there was not a house where there was not one dead, from the house of Pharaoh who sat on the throne to the prisoner in the dungeon. Where there was NO BLOOD, death came! Every firstborn in Egypt died! It made no difference about the inside of those houses when the death angel struck. It made no difference about the color of a man's face, how much he possessed, what his business or social standing was, or any other thing. Only one thing mattered, and that was that he had PUT THE BLOOD on the outside of the doorposts of his house.

I am saying to you, my friend, that when you and I come to die the only thing that will matter is that we have Jesus Christ as our Savior, Who gave His blood for our sins!

The Flood

There was no difference among the unsaved in the days of the Flood. Everyone outside the ark was drowned. If a man didn't get into the ark, he was drowned. If a woman didn't get into the ark, she was drowned. If a boy and girl didn't get into the ark, they were drowned. There was no difference between drunkard, harlot, leader, and judges: ALL who were on the outside of the ark perished! On the terrible night of God's Judgment, the only thing that mattered was to be safe inside the ark.

Sodom and Gomorrah

There was no difference in Sodom and Gomorrah when God Almighty rained down fire and brimstone from heaven and burned those wicked cities to the ground. The ruler of the city of Sodom died with the man who swept the streets. There was absolutely no difference. Everyone who failed to get out of those two condemned cities PERISHED in the fires of God's judgment wrath. They ignored the warning of the angels of God to flee from the iniquity of the city and its judgment. That is the way it will be on the Day of Judgment.

The Coming Judgment Revelation 6

In Revelation 6 God has painted us a picture of how the unsaved are going to react when His terrible judgment strikes. "And I beheld when He opened the sixth seal, and lo, there was a great earthquake, and the sun became black as sackcloth of hair, the moon became blood, and the stars of heaven fell unto the earth even as a fig tree casteth her untimely figs when she is shaken of a mighty wind. And the heaven departed as a scroll when it is rolled together, and every mountain and island were moved out of their places. And the kings of the earth, and the great men, and the rich men, and the chief captains, and the mighty men, and every bondman, and every free man hid themselves in the dens and in the rocks of the mountains and said to the mountains and rocks, fall on us and hide us from the Face of Him that sitteth on the throne and from the wrath of the Lamb, for the great Day of His Wrath is come, and who shall be able to stand?" That terrible Day of Judgment is coming! There will be NO DIFFERENCE: ALL will cry out for the rocks and mountains to fall on them! They did not seek shelter in the blood of the Lord Jesus. They spurned God's grace and God's Christ and God's great salvation, and they will cry out in that day! I have tried to tell you, friends, there is no difference among the unsaved. Without Christ, it will be JUDGMENT.

God's Spirit Will Not Always Strive

The third thing I have tried to tell you is that GOD'S SPIRIT WILL NOT ALWAYS STRIVE WITH YOU. The evidence is here tonight. The majority of people are saved by their sixteenth year. Beyond the sixteenth year, fewer come. Why? Somewhere down the line they grieve the Spirit of God away from their hearts. They keep saying NO to God, and they are not moved as young people are moved. I have tried to warn you. Some of you may go to church twenty more years, but you will never feel the Spirit of God as you once felt Him. Never again. It is dangerous to put off the Spirit of God! When He is moving in your heart, that is the time to come to Jesus. Right then and there.

I was pastor of a church in Atlanta for fourteen years. One day a call came asking me to go down and see a man dying in the cancer clinic in the city hospital. I went, and I found one of the hardest men I had ever dealt with in all my life. As I tried to talk with him about his soul, about his sins, about Jesus, about the Bible, he was as unconcerned as a cow munching grass in the field. He was totally unconcerned. Though he was dying, eaten up with cancer, on the brink of eternity, he had no thought of God, heaven, hell, or judgment upon his sins. He just brushed it out of his mind. Most people do. They run away from thinking. If I can get a man to think, he will come to Jesus! It is the only intelligent thing to do. But I couldn't get this man to think.

It was so tragic to see this dying man UNCONCERNED about eternity. I couldn't stand it. I walked out the door. I saw a woman I thought was his wife. Later I told my wife about this hardened man and his unconcern and that as I left I saw a woman I thought was his wife. She said, "That wasn't his wife. It was his true wife who called and asked you to go to see him. That was the other woman."

My heart ached. I understood why his heart was so hard. I understood then why his mind and soul were so unreachable. He was dying IN HIS SINS. He was hardened by the deceitfulness of SIN. God couldn't get through to him. He was encrusted with SIN. He could not cease from sinning. He was past feeling. Nobody would ever reach him. If an angel had come down from heaven, he couldn't have reached him.

One of the most solemn truths in the Bible, my friends, is that you can reject God and His Christ until you are beyond the reach of God! That is the Unpardonable Sin. It isn't God walking away and leaving you; it is that you have refused so long and have become so calloused and encrusted with SIN that God cannot get through to you. You have sent your own soul to hell! You have destroyed your own soul!

I tell you, God says, "My Spirit shall not always strive with man." When that man was a young man, like some of you here tonight, he had a tender heart. He heard the Gospel somewhere along the line. His heart was moved, but he didn't yield to the Spirit of God. That is why I say to you young people, "Don't grieve the Spirit of God. Don't put off receiving Christ." Years went by and that man came to the point that he could kick his wife out of house and home and take another woman AND DIE IN HIS SINS with that strange woman with him, never getting right with his wife, never getting right with God, never repenting of his sins. Somewhere along the line the Spirit of God left that man. I have tried to tell you that God says, "MY SPIRIT shall not always strive with man."

Man is Body, Soul, and Spirit

I want to remind you tonight that YOU CAN LOSE YOUR BODY, YOUR SOUL AND YOUR SPIRIT TO HELL. The Bible says that every human being is a tri-parte, three-fold, three-part being. Paul writes, "I pray God your spirit, soul and body be preserved blameless till the coming of the Lord Jesus Christ." I Thessalonians 5:23. You have a body, a soul and a spirit.

The Body

The Bible has much to say about our bodies. (If you read it, you may be surprised. If we could just get people to read the Bible, to know what God says!) The Greek word translated "body" is sos, and it means "a covering." That is what the body is, a covering. It is the house you are living in. One of these days the house is going to die and you will go out into eternity to meet God. The real YOU will still be alive when the house is destroyed. Remember that.

The Bible refers to natural men and spiritual men. A natural man is one who lets his natural appetites and passions control his body. A spiritual man is one who lets the Spirit of God control his body.

God tells us what we are to do with these bodies. He says to those who are His, "Yield your bodies as weapons of righteousness unto God and not as weapons of unrighteousness unto sin. " He says we are to glorify God in our bodies and in our spirits, which are God's.

I can use this tongue to curse God or to praise God. I can use these hands to handle the defiling and unclean or to handle the Word of God. I can use these feet to lead me in paths of righteousness for His Name's sake or in paths of unrighteousness and sin that lead to hell. We are to present our bodies "a living sacrifice holy and acceptable unto God, which is our reasonable service." Romans 12:1. My mind belongs to God. My ears belong to God. My tongue belongs to God. My hands, feet, entire being, belong to God. I have no business listening to the dirty and obscene. I have no business looking at that, which would offend God. I have no business talking about that, which would displease Him. I have no business letting my feet lead me where God would not want me to go. I have no business using these hands for anything but that which is holy and right in His eyes.

What are you doing with YOUR body? God sees all, all the time. He knows what we are doing with these bodies. The Apostle Paul said, "I beat my body black and blue and lead it around slavery lest I, having preached to others, myself should become a castaway." A preacher a castaway? Yes! Paul said he had to master his body, rule his body, keep his body under control. Everyone has passions, but no one has to yield to his passions. A man can control his base nature by the grace of God.

Paul says, "They that are Christ's have crucified THE FLESH with its passions and lusts." We see around us today men and women who have not crucified the flesh with its passions and lusts, and lust is damning the souls of men and women and boys and girls. May God help us to yield our bodies completely unto God, every member of our body a member of righteousness unto HIM.

You Can Lose Your Body to Hell

You can lose your body to hell. God speaks of hands, eyes, and feet being cast into FIRE. Mark 9. That is God's Word. Jesus speaks about the place "where the worm dieth not and the fire will never be quenched." You can lose your BODY to hell.

When I was pastor of a certain church, two doors from where I lived there was a young man, a preacher's son, unsaved. I made up my mind that I would lead him to Christ, if I could. I went to see him three times. I went to his home. I prayed with him and his wife and children, but he didn't accept Christ. We had a great tent meeting, and souls were being saved. He came three nights but never yielded to the Lord. He went his way.

After the revival meeting I went out of town, and when I got back my wife told me he was in the hospital with double pneumonia. I went to see him thinking that maybe this was the time. I walked into the room, and there he was under an oxygen tent. It is pitiful when someone has to heave for his breath, trying to get his breath, having to use an oxygen tent to live. I put my mouth down to the little aperture where you can reach in and touch them or speak to them, and I took his hand. He was gasping for breath. His mother, wife and children were standing around. I said, "Will you right now take Christ for your Savior?" He squeezed my hand with the little strength he had left and gasped a very weak, "Yes." He died the next day.

You say, "Brother Hendley, aren't you glad he was saved!"

I say, "IF he was saved." God knows I wanted him to be saved. That's why I visited him. I wanted him saved, with all my soul! I hope I will meet him in Heaven. He may have been saved, for Jesus saved the dying thief. But I question deathbed repentances. MAYBE a man can forget God all his life and live wickedly and live rejecting God and His Son and the Gospel and the Bible and prayer and soul winning and the work of the Lord. MAYBE he can live a lifetime neglecting spiritual things and come down to his last gasp under an oxygen tent and squeeze the preacher's hand and say "Yes, I take Jesus," with his body filled with drugs and his mind confused as he dies. MAYBE he can get through, I don't know. I wouldn't want to gamble on it. I wouldn't want to take that risk. The best way is to make sure you are saved BEFORE this time comes. Everyone is going to spend eternity either in heaven or hell. This matter is too important to wait until the last minute. Have you trusted Jesus as your Savior, and have you yielded your body to Him?

You Can Lose Your Soul to Hell

You can lose your SOUL to hell. Many people do not think about their souls; they think only about the body. But you have more than a body, friend. You have something far more precious than a body; you have a soul! What is the soul?

In the Image of God

When God created Adam and Eve He said, "Let us make man in Our image and after Our likeness." So God created man in His own image. Male and female created He them, and God breathed into their nostrils the breath of life and man became a living soul.

"Made in the image of God." What does that mean? Physical image? No. We are not made in the image of God physically. Do not think that God looks like you and me. The image of God is not physical. God is an essentially SPIRITUAL Being, and the spiritual world is more real than this world. This world is going to pass away. The spiritual world will abide forever! Remember that.

So you have a soul. You are made in "the image of God." What is there about you that is LIKE GOD? For an image is a likeness, and if we are in the image of God we are like Him in some way. YOU ARE A LIVING PERSONALITY WHOLLY APART FROM A PHYSICAL BODY, capable of will and reason and motion. You will survive the shock of death and LIVE ON FOREVER.

You are a living personality, apart from your body. The Real You---that living, thinking, feeling, knowing personality will LIVE

ETERNALLY. When God created you in your mother's womb, he created your living SOUL in your living BODY. That is when A SOUL is created---not at birth, but at conception. You became a personality that will NEVER DIE. Think about eternity: You will be ALIVE ten million years from now, ten billion years from now, forever, and forever, and forever! As long as GOD lives, you and I are destined to live. When God created you, He created you for eternity. The Real You and I will never die, because THE SOUL will never die. Your body will die, but your soul will never, never, never, never, never, never die. The soul is the Real You, the person that looks out of those eyes, hears through those ears, moves about in that body, moves those hands and feet.

Many of you young people are being taught in school the fallacy that man is an animal. Man is not an animal. There never was a dog that beat his breast and said, "God, be merciful to me a sinner." God never made a chicken in the image of God. God never made a cow in the image of God. God never made a bear in the image of God. Only MAN was created in God's own image. Man is the crown of God's creation, and it is blasphemy against the God of heaven and the God of the Bible to say that man is an ANIMAL. Dogs don't go to heaven when they die. Chickens don't go to heaven when they die. They do not repent of sin; they have no consciousness of God. They do not have souls in the sense that man has a soul. Never! When they die, they are dead. God created man to live forever.

The Greek word for "man" is anthropos, and it comes from a word that means "the upward looker." Man looks UPWARD. An animal looks downward. Everything it needs it finds here on earth. But not man. You don't find all you need on earth. Your soul needs

GOD. You need the things of eternity. You need salvation. You need eternal life. Your soul---that thinking, feeling, emotional, willing, purposing, acting part of you---will LIVE ON when your body has returned to dust. Your SOUL was created for ETERNITY. That is why the Lord Jesus said, "What shall it profit a man if he gain the whole world and LOSE his own soul?"

Suppose I could gain all the wealth that is here in this city with its tremendous businesses and banks. Suppose I could obtain and enjoy all that is in the world, everything this world has, for ten, twenty, thirty, forty, fifty, sixty, seventy, eighty years. AND THEN DIE WITHOUT CHRIST; I'd be a fool. Why? Because God's Word says I have A SOUL THAT WILL LIVE FOREVER. More important than owning the world is getting your soul saved for eternity, to go out and meet God, to ntained on the other side."

When Jesus was dying, He said, "Father, into Thy hands I commend My---" Body? No. "I commend my soul?" No. "I commend my SPIRIT." What did He mean? "Father, You and I have been in unbroken contact with each other. Let it be maintained on into the next world."

Your spirit is the most important part of you. I read in this Bible, "The spirits of just men made perfect in heaven." It means SAVED men, whose spirits are made perfect in heaven.

I also read in this Bible of "spirits in prison." There is a prison house for lost spirits, where they spend eternity! I don't want to join that crowd. I don't want my spirit to be in jail forever and ever. That is where your spirit will be if you die without Christ.

Let's go back to the text, Psalm 21:1, "My God, My God, why hast Thou forsaken Me?"

Forsaken of Parents

It is an awful thing to be forsaken of your parents. I preached over the radio one night from our tabernacle. Monday morning I had a telephone call from a lady. She said, "I am part-owner of a house for girls who have fallen into trouble. There is a sixteen-year-old girl here from a prominent Atlanta family. She has fallen into sin. When her parents found out her condition, that a baby was to be born, they kicked her out of house and home instead of helping her when she needed help so much. They said, 'you have disgraced us. You have dishonored our name. You don't belong to us anymore. We don't want any more to do with you,' and they utterly forsook her. In her desperation she came here for her baby to be born. I am a trained nurse. I was with her last night when the time came for your broadcast and she asked that I tune in. Preacher, to make a long story short, we tuned in and two souls were saved at the close of your broadcast. We both knelt and received Jesus as our Saviour and Lord."

What MADE that girl, forsaken of her mother, forsaken of her father, because of her sin, turn to me and to my broadcast that particular night? It was because she remembered a word found in the Psalms: "When my mother and father forsake me, THE LORD will take me up." Psalm 27:10. And the Lord did take her up! He saved her! I learned later that He straightened up her life. God can do that. WONDERFUL GOD!

It is a terrible thing to be forsaken of parents, to be forsaken by those you love. But it is terrible beyond words to be FORSAKEN of the Living God, and THIS is what we have in the text tonight: "My God, My God, why hast Thou forsaken Me?" This is the cry of somebody forsaken of God. That Somebody was the very Son of God, the Lord Jesus.

You remember that at the beginning of His ministry Jesus was popular. Everybody rushed after Him because of His tremendous miracles. But as He began to tell them about the cost of discipleship and walking with God, they didn't want to pay the price for a holy life. So they began to leave Him. Many turned away.

Finally Jesus became the loneliest Man this world has ever known. He was forsaken of His family. They said He was beside Himself (crazy). He was forsaken of His own people, the Jews. "He came unto His own and His own received Him not." He was forsaken finally of His disciples. As He went into the shadows of the cross, His disciples forsook Him and fled. Through it all He foresaw that everyone was going to forsake Him. He had no human being to comfort Him or be with Him in His agony. He told them plainly, "I am going to Jerusalem and be betrayed into the hands of sinners and Gentiles. You all are going to forsake Me and flee from Me." Then He said something glorious: "But My Father is with Me." And as He approached the Cross and every human being left Him, He had Somebody more important than all human beings: He had God His Father with Him.

Beloved, when I come to die, I want GOD with Me. I want God with me! There is an hour coming in my life when my wife cannot go with me, nor my son, nor daughter, nor friends, nobody on earth. I WANT GOD THERE. I want to be able to say with David, "Yea, though I walk through the valley of the shadow of death, I will fear no evil, for THOU ARE WITH ME."

Jesus faced death with confidence because God was with Him. He was nailed to a cross at nine o'clock in the morning, and during those first three agonizing hours His Father was with Him. He had GOD to sustain Him. The first cry from the cross was, "Father, forgive them, for they know not what they do."

But, my friends hear me. At twelve o'clock noon a terrible darkness covered the earth, particularly over Calvary's cross, and there came from the lips of the Divine Sufferer an awful scream, "My God, My God! Why hast THOU forsaken Me?" And from twelve noon until three, JESUS CHRIST BECAME A GOD-FORSAKEN SOUL, THAT YOU AND I MIGHT NEVER BE FORSAKEN OF GOD! In those three hours He became A LOST SOUL. He tasted DEATH, and death means HELL. For every man! In place of every man! In every man's stead! That means that if you receive Him as your Savior and Lord, your Substitute, your Sin-bearer, you yourself will not have to taste death. He says, "Whosoever believeth in Me shall never die." John 6. He has already tasted it FOR YOU. THAT DAY HE TOOK YOUR PLACE. HE TOOK MY PLACE.

This was foreshadowed in Psalm 22, "My God, my God, why hast Thou forsaken Me? Why art Thou so far from helping Me and from the words of My roaring? O my God, I cry in the daytime but Thou hearest not." That is what souls are screaming in hell today, the same thing Jesus cried from the cross. That is what you will scream forever, the cry of the damned in Psalm 22. "O my God, I cry in the daytime but Thou answerest not, in the night season, and am not silent. You do not hear us in hell! You do not answer lost souls, day nor night."

He tells His physical agony: "I am poured out like water and all My bones are out of joint. My heart is like wax; it is melted within Me. My tongue cleaveth to My jaws. Thou hast brought Me into the dust of death. Deliver My soul from the sword, my darling [which means His soul] from the power of the dog. Save Me from the lion's mouth."

When Jesus died, He took my hell for me. I am not going there! YOU don't have to go when you receive Him as your Savior and Lord. But hear me, my friend! If you reject Jesus Christ and shut Him out of your life, you will become a GOD-forsaken soul! What Jesus went through on that cross, YOU will have to go through, not for three hours but through the ages of an unending ETERNITY. You will be LOST, damned, forsaken of God Almighty and loved ones and friends. Oh! The loneliness of an eternity without GOD and without help, throughout the ages to come!

This is profound. This is the Heart of the Gospel. The only thing that matters then is to accept Jesus as your Savior and Lord. HE HAS ALREADY TAKEN YOUR HELL, the punishment for your sins. He became a God-forsaken soul in your stead. YOU CAN NEVER BE LOST when you trust Jesus Christ as your Savior and Lord and receive Him into your heart.

DON'T WAIT TOO LATE.

I was preaching in my church one night and gave the invitation, and among those who came was a woman. She received Christ, then turned to me and said, "My husband is back there. I wish you would ask him to come tonight." I turned and continued the invitation. Finally a big, strong man walked down the aisle and knelt beside this woman and came to Jesus. About three weeks later I baptized him.

One night he was coming home from a large hotel in Atlanta where he worked as an engineer. He had been working many hours overtime and in driving home he evidently fell asleep at the wheel, for a bus operator, going back into Atlanta on his last run said, "I saw that car veering toward me. I could not get out of the way, and there was a head-on crash. This man was killed.

His body was brought back to the church where just three weeks before he had accepted Jesus. I'll never forget that after the funeral service his father and wife and children came up to the casket. That old daddy bent over his boy, hot tears dripping down on his cold cheeks, and he sobbed out, "My son! My Son!" in his agony. I patted him on the back and said, "You don't have to worry. That is not the wail of eternal separation; it is just the cry of temporary separation. You are going to meet your boy again. He got in, just in time."

His son had made contact with God JUST IN TIME. He didn't know that within three weeks he would be wheeled into that church in a casket and be taken out to the cemetery and be buried. He had trusted in Jesus, IN TIME, by just three weeks.

My friend, if you are not sure you are saved, you can be NOW.

The Bible says, "Whosoever shall call upon the Name of the Lord shall be saved." Romans 10:13. If you believe Jesus loved you and died to pay for your sins, invite Him into your heart. When you RECEIVE HIM, God says you are saved. Saving faith is that inward, total confidence in Jesus that relies on Him alone for salvation. Will you trust Him now? Will you do it? God bless you.

Precious Memory

"I remember the first time I heard of Jess Hendley. It was during a tent revival in Toccoa, Georgia when I was just a boy. My father came home one day excited about hearing a dynamic preacher who preached the gospel in such a passionate way that souls were streaming down the "sawdust trail" to accept Christ during this tent meeting revival.

I never shall forget the excitement that next night as that I, as a little boy along with the family, went to hear brother Jess preach. He was lightning and thunder all in one preacher!

During those days I could have never imagined that I would later answer the call to pastor and one Sunday Morning see Dr. Hendley along with his wife Louise come down the aisle of Rehoboth Baptist Church, hug my neck and say, "We want to join the church and have you as our pastor." Wow, I thought, my preaching better really improve if I intend to pastor one of the modern day "heroes of the faith." I can truthfully tell you that Jess was a pastor's best friend and tremendous mentor.

Through the years that followed and even into his senior years many souls were won to Christ through his preaching and radio ministry across the nation as he continued to bear fruit for the kingdom of God.

THE WORLD CRISIS AND THE ONLY WAY OUT

I know that you will enjoy reading the wonderful compilation of his sermons, but I also pray the God's Spirit will give you a glimpse of the passion and power that Dr. Jess Hendley possessed as he preached."

Dr. Richard G. Lee
Founding Pastor, First Redeemer Church
President/Speaker, There's Hope America

Revival promo picture from 1970s.

LAZARUS – AFTER DEATH WHAT?

It was my request that we put on this Sunday School night, tonight, and the reason I did it is because in our city wide meetings we do not have a chance to come to the individual churches and reach the people we could reach in the Sunday Schools there, so it was my request, my desire, because we love young people, we love boys and girls, men and women and those who have Sunday Schools that, otherwise, we might not be able to reach and that's the reason why we put on this Sunday School night, tonight, and I want you to listen to me carefully please as I speak to you on the 16th Chapter of Luke and I remind you that these are the words of The Lord Jesus Christ. "There was a certain rich man, which was clothed in purple and fine linen, and fared sumptuously every day: And there was a certain beggar named Lazarus, which was laid at his gate, full of sores, and desiring to be fed with the crumbs which fell from the rich man's table: moreover, the dogs came and licked his sores. And it came to pass, that the beggar died, and was carried by the angels into Abraham's bosom: the rich man also died, and was buried: And in hell he lift up his eyes, being in torments, and he seeth Abraham afar off, Lazarus in his bosom. And he cried and said, Father Abraham, have mercy on me, and send Lazarus, that he may dip the tip of his finger in water, and cool my tongue; for I am tormented in this flame. But Abraham said, Son remember that thou in thy lifetime received thy good things, and likewise Lazarus evil things: but now he is comforted and thou art tormented. And beside all this, between us and you there is a great gulf fixed: So that they which would pass from hence to you cannot; neither can they pass to us, that would come thence. Then he said, I pray thee therefore, father, that thou wouldest send him to my father's house: For I have five brethren; that he may testify unto them, lest they also come into this place of torment. But Abraham saith unto him, they have Moses and the prophets," They've got the Bible to warn them, "let them hear them." Let them listen to the prophets of God and the Bible and "he said Nay, Father Abraham: but if one went unto them from the dead, they will repent. And he said unto him, if they hear not Moses and the prophets," if a man or woman or boy or girl will not listen to the Word of God, "neither will they be persuaded, though one rose from the dead."

So tonight I want to speak to you on the subject AFTER DEATH, WHAT? A subject that is of vital consequences to every one of us here. MY text is found in Job 14:14, "If a man die, does he live again?" Now those are the words of Job. The word again is in italics indicating it is not in the Hebrew text. What Job was doing was raising the question, if a man dies, is he still alive or is he just blotted out? Does he cease to exist? That faces every one of us when we come to die. We want to know is there any life beyond the grave. Back during the Korean war the Chaplains tell us that there came to them soldiers, just before they went into the conflict, into battle, into danger, and said Chaplain tell us, "Is there life beyond the grave?" If a bullet gets us or shrapnel gets us, or bombs get us, or a bayonet and we are killed will we still be alive, is there anything to this mortality business, is there anything to this life beyond the grave business, tell us, we want to know the truth.

Now the Bible answers that question in the affirmative, there is a life beyond the grave. We open our Bibles and we read that Enoch walked with God and He was not for God took him. God removed him from this world to the next world, and there is evidence of a life beyond the grave. At the burning bush God says to Moses "I am the God of Abraham, the God of Isaac and the God of Jacob." They were already dead and Jesus commenting on that passage says that God is not the God of the Dead, but the God of the Living; and He makes this profound statement for all who live under Him, which means, that everybody that's ever lived is alive today. Adam is alive right now, Eve is alive, Cain and Abel are alive, Isaiah is alive, Paul the Apostle is alive, every person God ever created from Adam's time to this moment is in conscious existence in another world right this minute. They have not been blotted out, they haven't ceased to exist, they are in conscious existence in another world according to that statement.

Job answered his own question when he said, "I know that my redeemer liveth and when the worms have destroyed this body yet apart from my flesh shall my eyes see God and not another." He knew that when his body was in the grave and his body was devoured by worms he would not be in the grave, he wasn't going to a grave, he was going to be looking in God's face in the land beyond.

David when his little baby died, bent over the crib of his little dead baby boy and he sobbed out "I shall go to him but he shall not return to me." He knew that his baby was alive, his body was in the crib before him, but he knew he would meet his baby in another world because he was a real child of the living God. In Psalm 23, which I suppose has been one of the most comforting Psalms in regard to death for the people of God down through the ages, in the last verse we read "Surely goodness and mercy shall follow me all the days of my life" and wouldn't there have been a tragedy had there been a period put there, but the Psalmist said life is no dead end street and he goes on singing when life's little day is over "I'm going to live in God's big house forever," and he knew there is a life beyond the grave.

You remember when Stephen was being stoned to death by his enemies he looked yonder toward the heavens and saw the heavens opened and Jesus standing at the right hand of God and he sobbed out "Lord Jesus receive my spirit" and we have the record that Jesus Christ, ordinarily stated his seating by the Father's Right Hand stood to his feet to welcome this soul of his dying martyr being crushed to death on the streets of earth down below.

Then again Jesus, one day just before He died went to the Northern most part of the land of Palestine to Mt. Hermon the highest peak there, and suddenly as He took with Him, Peter, James, and John, He was transfigured before them and He set upon Himself the glory which He had with the Father before the world wide and there stood Moses, and Elijah speaking concerning His decease, His death which was to be accomplished at Jerusalem, may I remind you that Moses had been dead fifteen hundred years and there he is very much alive. May I remind you that Elijah was caught up in a chariot of Glory five hundred years previous to this time, but there he is very much alive.

These passages and many others, in the Word of God, teaches without a shadow of a question of a doubt that you and I are not going to be blotted out, when our bodies die we're going to be alive in another world. Death isn't all, after death there is life in the land beyond. Now if that be true, if there is a life beyond the grave, if we never die to our real personalities and souls and only our bodies shall die and we will be still alive in conscious existence beyond the grave the question comes to us, where do we go and what is our condition going to be? The Bible divides people in the saved and the unsaved, where do the saved go when they die? Where do the unsaved go when they die? Now the Lord answers in the story I read to you tonight. He tells us about two men, a rich man and a beggar. The very extreme of human society. You see these men in this world, and then we see them come down to die that's as far as you and I can go, we can't go beyond the grave. Now Jesus pulls back the veil and shows us the soul of a saved man and the soul of an unsaved man going into eternity to meet God. Now let's look very carefully, exactly, at what Jesus has to say. It's going to happen to every one of us saved and unsaved under this tent when we come to die. He said "there was a certain rich man clothed in purple and fine linen, faring sumptuously every day and a certain beggar named Lazarus laid at his gate full of sores desiring to be fed with the crumbs which fell from the rich man's table; moreover the dogs came and licked his sores."

And you and I desire to go home with that wealthy man, see him living luxuriously, everything his heart could desire and see that miserable beggar at his gate, nobody cares for him, no roof over his head, miserable, and the dogs come to the body filled with running sores and begging the very crumbs that fell from the rich man's table to keep the little flicker of life going. I say if you and I saw the rich man and beggar, I say to you which had you rather be. Ah, you say without thinking that's easy, give me the life of the rich man but let's wait a minute, let's see the rich man go on and die and go to hell. Let's see the beggar die and be carried into comfort and bliss. I ask you now who had you rather be, you say preacher I'd rather have the life of the rich man here and the life of the beggar in the other world, but that's impossible, you're only one personality, you have only one life to live, one death to die, and one eternity to spend and it's impossible for you to be changed whatsoever.

We read, "It came to pass, that the beggar died." Is that all? That's not all for the beggar, it wasn't all for the rich man, and death is not going to be all for me and death is not going to be all for you. "It came to pass that the beggar died and was carried by the angels into Abraham's bosom." The bosom is a place of comfort. Abraham was a father of believers; Abraham's bosom is a place where believers were comforted. May I remind you friends that when this beggar died he was carried by the angels into paradise, into Abraham's bosom. And if you should tell me tonight, if I should die, if this heart stopped beating while I'm on this pulpit stand, that the angels of heaven are waiting to bear my soul into God's presence and into glory and comfort and bliss, I'd be willing to die, but if you told me the demons of hell are waiting to drag my soul down in the everlasting torments, believe me, I wouldn't want to die.

When the beggar died, he had the angels of God waiting to carry his soul into Abraham's bosom into the comfort and bliss. We read, "The rich man also died". Yes, we do sweat for riches in this world but here is an unsaved rich man. May I remind you a man can't sign a check sixty seconds after he is dead and the only man that God ever called to that Jesus tells us about is found in Luke the 12th Chapter. He was a wealthy farmer, he had his barns filled with plenty, a wealthy man. He had a big crop coming on he didn't know what to do. He sat down and decided "I know what I'll do, I'll tear down all these barns, I'll build larger barns, I'll fill them up and then I'll say to my soul, Soul take thine ease eat, drink and be merry for thou hast much goods laid up for many years," but God said, "Thou fool, many years," you are not going to live a year, you're not going to live a month, you're not going to live a week, you're not going to live twenty-four hours, "tonight shall thou soul be required of thee." Tonight you're going to die and then whose shall these things be which thou hast provided.

We read "the rich man also died and was buried." Did you notice Jesus didn't say the beggar was buried? They tell me that in Jesus day there were so many beggars in the East and they were so despised, nobody cared about beggars and when they died they didn't take the trouble to bury them, they simple flung their bodies on the side of the road for the dogs and vultures to eat. We do not read that the beggar was buried. We read that the rich man had a very ornate funeral even when his soul had dropped already into hell. We read the rich man died and was buried and in hell lifted up his eyes being in torment.

Brother Hendley, you're not going to stand in that pulpit and tell us you're an old-fashioned believer in hell, nobody believes in hell anymore. Preachers don't preach about hell anymore; theological students don't study about hell anymore. Why brother Hendley, don't you know that's old fogeyism, the old preachers used to preach about hell and scare people, but nobody does that anymore, we're living in an enlightened age and we've gotten rid of hell. I'm not quite so sure about it. The Lord Jesus said hell, you know the Bible teaches it all the way through.

I remember back yonder when I first started preaching I had the old-fashioned idea that the business of a preacher was to preach the Bible. So I began to study the Bible and I thought I read something about hell, that people who don't love Christ, men, women, boys and girls, were going to hell, and be tormented and burned forever and ever. I thought I saw it there and so I went into a revival meeting yonder in Atlanta, in those early days as a young preacher, and one night I thought well, if all boys and girls and men and women are all going to hell without Christ I ought to try to warn them and try to get them saved, so I preached on hell.

The preacher took me to task about it, the only time I've ever had a man to challenge my preaching. He said I'm no hell preacher I believe in preaching only the love of God and not preaching anything about hell, I don't believe there is a hell. Well, I lived to see that man announce hell within a years' time. He preached on it because his people wanted the truth and within two years' time God called him into eternity. I never will forget going home that night, I said, if I made a horrible mistake, I was just a young preacher, I said if I've made a horrible mistake and I got out here and told people that there is a hell and there isn't any hell. I went back to my Bible and begin to search it again and what do you think I found. I found it all over the pages of the Bible.

Isaiah said, "Hell from beneath is moved for thee to meet thee at thy coming," you remember that don't you. Job said hell and destruction is ever full, David said the wicked shall be turned into hell and all the nations that forget God. King Solomon said he that be reproved and hardens his neck shall suddenly be destroyed in that without remedy. The Apostle Paul in the New Testament said the Lord Jesus shall be revealed from heaven in flaming fire, taking vengeance on them that know not God and have they not the Gospel who shall be punished with everlasting destruction, from the presence of the Lord and the glory of His power for He comes to give life to his saints.

John the beloved apostle, the Apostle of love was the one who warned men of the lake of fire into which every unsaved man, woman, boy or girl shall be cast and spend eternity, and can you imagine my friends, in my research in the Bible on this tremendous theme of the lostness of loss souls in hell, that the most solemn words I've found that fell from any lips, fell from the tenderest lips this world has ever known from the lips of Jesus, it is He that warns of the place of torment. It is He that speaks of a place where your worm will never die and your fire shall never be quenched. It is Jesus that warns it is better to pluck out your eyes and chop off your hands and your feet than to let your eyes, and hands and feet lead you into sin and lead you into hell. We read Jesus saying the rich man died and was buried and instantly, not off yonder in some far-off judgment day, or some thousand years, millenarianism away, but instantly in hell he lifted up his eyes being in torment.

Brother Hendley, you're not going to stand there in that pulpit and tell us you're on old fashioned believer in torment, don't you know we've gotten rid of it, nobody believes, men, women, boys and girls who die without Christ are going to be tormented, why if preachers believed that, they'd preach it and if theological professors believed that they'd teach it above everything else. If men, women, boys and girls in Flint, without Christ are going into hell to be tormented don't you know they ought to be warned about it? Surely it isn't so. Beloved friends Jesus said torment. I've tried to be honest with the Bible, I've tried as best I know how to be honest with the Word of God, I have no traffic, no trunk with anybody that trifles with the plain statements of the Word.

If the Bible is the Word of God it ought to be preached just as it is. I believe that with all my soul and yonder is a man whom I've dreamed to be a man honest at the genetic of scripture and so in his old age he wrote a book one time and he said there's no such thing as torment. I went back to my Greek Testament, one more time and checked that Greek word and these preachers who are here will recognize that, that word is Basanois, BASANOIS, it's in the plural and it means torture. This man was tortured the minute he died. God's Word teaches that people who shut God out of their lives and refuse God's mercy and God's grace and God's Son after He died on the Cross for them are going into torture in the next world the minute their heart stops beating. It's a teaching of the Word of God and I say to you, my friends, I've seen all the pain I want to see in this world.

Yonder in East Point, Ga. a very Godly woman who died 70 years of age of cancer, she said I've suffered seventeen months of that awful dread disease. One Sunday afternoon my wife and I were down visiting her and she looked at me and said preacher you think it very strange that I sometimes consider taking my own life. I said in astonishment, I was a young Christian, I couldn't think of a

Christian wanting to take her life, I said what do you mean? She said I think about trying to get my husband out of the room so I can get to the gas over there and take my life. I said woman why do you want to take your life? She looked at me with that pitiful, suffering face and she said Preacher if hell is anything like the awful suffering; with this cancer I've been going through these seventeen months, she said you preachers ought to go out into the streets and scream to the top of your voice and warn people about that awful place.

I want to say to you my friends the rich man died and was buried and in hell he lifted up his eyes being in torment said Jesus and he seeth Abraham afar off and Lazarus in his bosom and he cried and said Father Abraham, let me call your attention to that word Father, earthly relationships do not exist in that lost world. I would not like for my precious wife for whom I've lived with for 28 years to die without my Christ and in hell lift her face calling for me, her husband, and I'd be yonder in heaven unable to reach her. I wouldn't like for my 22-year-old daughter to die without my Christ and go to hell and there lift her pitiful face in the flames of hell begging for dad and dad be unable to reach her, I wouldn't like for my 20-year-old son yonder in Italy tonight to die without my Christ and yonder go to hell and lift his little face in the flames of hell screaming for his daddy that could help in this world but be unable to help him there. Earth relationships do not exist in that world.

Dads and mothers get your children, your family and wives your husbands and husbands your wives, children your parents before it's too late. God's Word says that they're lost without the Lord Jesus and going to this very terrible, terrible world. It's terrible, Father Abraham have mercy on me. May I remind you my friends that God has no mercy on souls in that lost world. There is no mercy there whatsoever. God's Word says after death judgment, not after death mercy. God's Word says that anyone who despises His Word and shuts God and Christ out of their lives shall die without mercies. I was in Dallas, Texas in a revival meeting some years ago. While I was there a terrible murder took place. It seems that the sheriff and his deputy had an argument over vacation and the deputy went away for a little bit, he came back and resumed the argument with the sheriff and the sheriff grew angry and grabbed his gun and shot the man. That deputy was on the ground, in his agony, with a bullet in his body and he cried out "Sheriff have mercy on me, don't shoot me, don't kill me" and that man stood over him with that gun with no mercy in his heart and he pulled that trigger until he emptied every bullet into that man's body while he was screaming for mercy.

God said the man, woman, boy or girl that shuts His Son out of their lives and refuses His Great Salvation and Sacrifice shall die without mercy. There is no mercy in that lost world. Father Abraham have mercy on me and send Lazarus that he may dip the tip of his finger in water and cool my tongue, I'm tormented in this flame. May I call your attention to the fact, my friends, hell must be a very dreadful place, if a drop of water will give you any ease whatsoever.

Notice this man didn't ask to get out of hell, he knows nobody ever gets out. Notice he didn't ask that he shouldn't suffer, he knows that anybody that dies without Christ and goes to hell must suffer. All he asks for was a momentary, temporary, alleviation of his pain and agony and he didn't even get that. Then let us learn the lesson from Jesus' Words, that hell is a place of unrelieved pain and I say to you again I've see all the agony and pain I want to see in this present world. Father Abraham send Lazarus and let him dip the tip of his finger in water and cool my tongue I'm tormented in this flame.

Brother Hendley you're not going to stand in that pulpit and tell us you're an old-fashioned believer in fire. You don't actually believe that men, women, boys and girls who shut God and Christ out of their lives and refuse His great Salvation are going to burn. You don't actually believe there is a burning hell, do you preacher? The Lord Jesus said FIRE. The Lord Jesus said FLAME.

John Wesley who had one of the greatest minds I suppose in American History used to stand before his audiences and shake them when he said my friends can you stick your finger in the flame of a candle and hold it there. No, how can you stand your whole body cast into the flame of hell that Jesus speaks about. Charles G. Finney used to speak of the lake of fire into which the unsaved would be cast know ye tongues of pain for lashes of burning sores for ever and ever. And Jonathan Edwards, everyone knows who does any reading at all that Edward's had one of the greatest intellects in the history of the world and is one of the greatest preachers with that intellect. Jonathan Edwards used to shake his audiences when he said my friends hell is a place where sinners hands, and eyes, and mouth, and loins, and entire being is filled with roaring, melting fire and somebody yells imagination.

May I say to you my friends I've studied this Bible twenty-eight years on that world out yonder we're going into and I'm saying to you, there is no imagination that can devise the doom of those who shut Jesus out of their lives and refuse His bloodied Salvation as the

Bible warns about in the Holy Book of God. It's a terrible thing to be lost, without God and without hope.

Now this man begged that Abraham would send Lazarus and dip the tip of his finger in water and cool his tongue he said, "For I am tormented in this flame." Did he get an answer to this prayer? Oh, no, prayers are not answered in hell. Son, Remember! These are two terrible words, Son, Remember, well what does that mean? It means that you're going to take your memory with you when you die and what a hell memory is going to be to those who rejected Jesus. What a hell memory is going to be.

My wife had a girl friend who had a sister; a beautiful woman. She prostituted her beauty for purposes of sin and it finally got her down like sin is going to get everybody down. You have to pay the piper friends. The old skeletons come out of the closet and the chickens come home to roost and someday you have to sit down and look your sins in the face when you meet God. Remember that please, Son Remember. When this precious girl was hospitalized and they gave her medicine and everything else, you can pour medicine all you please down a sinner's heart and it's not going to reach the conscience and reach the memory, it didn't do any good and finally she tried to take her life and her sister got to her just in time to save her and brought her to my home.

I dealt with that miserable woman on the couch in my living room for three hours and finally I said to her, why is it you tried to take your life and she looked at me and she said Preacher I can't sleep at night. She said when I try to sleep I see my sins at the foot of my bed. I stare them in the face but I can't sleep and she said I get up and hang curtains and rearrange furniture and think and preacher you can't live without sleep. And I said oh, what a hell memory is going to be. Abraham said Son Remember, during your lifetime you received good things you had your chance and Lazarus likewise evil things but now he is comforted and thou art tormented, and besides all this between us and you there is a great gulf fixed, now may I call your attention to that gulf that separates the saved from the unsaved in that world.

One night one of our faithful preachers was preaching on the great gulf fixed that separates the saved from the unsaved in the other world. He raised this statement at the close of his message and he said, sitting here tonight is husband and wife and wife you're saved and husband you're unsaved, if you die tonight, wife you'd be on the heaven side of the gulf and husband you'd be on the hell side of the gulf. Wife you can't cross to the husband's and husband you can't cross to the wife's, you'd be like that separated through the ages of eternity.

A man dropped his head like he was shot through the heart, he was speaking directly to him his wife was a Christian, he wasn't. He wasn't saved. On the way home they didn't say very much. He didn't say very much. They retired, he tossed and tumbled with those words burning in his soul, burning in his conscious, finally about two in the morning he said to his wife who was praying for him, wife did that preacher tell the truth? She said what do you mean? He said if you and I died tonight you'd be on the heaven side of the gulf and I'd be on the hell side of the gulf, I couldn't cross to you and you couldn't cross to me and we'd be separated forever, did he tell the truth? She said yes husband he told the truth. Wait a minute, she flipped on the light and turned to her old worn Bible and turned to Luke 16:26 and read it "Between us and you there is a great gulf fixed", he told the truth husband. The man started crying and he said wife we've lived together all these years and we've raised our family together I love you and I know you love me and I don't want to be separated from you forever I want to get on your side of the gulf. She said let's pray and they stumbled down on their knees beside their bed at two o'clock in the morning, that man wept his way into the Arms of Jesus Christ and accepted Christ as his Savior and crossed the gulf before it was too late.

Next morning he scarce let the preacher get to his study when he went bursting through the preacher's study door saying preacher I'm saved. At two o'clock this morning I got on my wife's part of the gulf, I'm saved. He crossed that gulf just in time, but oh my friends, death is going to seal that gulf and you'll never be able to cross it. Never be able to cross it.

Jesus said that this man says between us and you, Abraham said between us and you, we're on the same side and you're on the other side, between us and you there is a great gulf fixed, and I sometimes think that word fixed is the most terrible word in all the Bible. It is a Greek word in the perfect tense and it means something that's become fixed in times past and remains in an unalterable state of fixture that you can't change. Fixed, somebody has well said that dying times fixing time and that's exactly right. The wonderful Isaac Nupert, the famous infidel, when he came to die and friends said do you want us to pray for you, as he realized his lost condition, it won't do any good. In Hell I'd be a happy soul but a billion years will not bring me to the end of my suffering any more than one short hour and he died screaming oh the insufferable pangs of hell, oh eternity, eternity. It's an awful thing to be lost and to go into that world of burning.

Yonder one time over the radio came a phone call a few years ago from a precious wife, she was crying, she said preacher will you come down here and try to lead my husband to Christ. This man or husband, was an electrician. He had gone into a newly, painted and built, building and evidently gas had escaped and he started to light his blow torch and there was a terrible explosion, his garments were burned off from his shoulders to his feet, he fell groveling in pain on the floor, his buddy heard him screaming, he rushed in and picked him up and put him in the car and rushed him to Grady Hospital. He died three days later and this was the second day when she called me.

I went down to see him and when I started in the door there stood the wife weeping, do what you can preacher and there was a young daughter, do what you can for my daddy. I walked in the room and there he was over that tent like affair with which they treat burns. I took one look at his body and I hope, I hope I'll never see anybody in that condition again. Literally, chunks of roasted flesh had fallen off his bones. How he was living I'll never know but I saw he was still conscience with beads of perspiration on his face. I bent over him, I said, oh fellow, are you saved. He said preacher I'm not going to lie to you I'm not a Christian. Well, I said let's call on the Lord, He'll save you right now. So I bowed my head and started praying for him and to my amazement he stopped me and said not now preacher I'm in too great pain, I'm in too great agony. You'll have to leave me now preacher and he begin to be emotionally upset and the loved ones and the interns and the doctors came rushing in to help him and what can a preacher do.

A man in that condition, you can't get through to his mind and there was nothing for me to do but to leave him and that man lay there and died the next day without God and hope on his own testimony. He said to me as he was dying "I'm not a Christian." When I walked away from that man and out of the hospital and looked up at God's stars I said Oh God, if hell is anything like what that man is going through with I don't want to go and I certainly don't want anybody else to go.

And I'm saying to you my friends tonight don't you rest, don't you tell anything else, don't you let anything enter your mind until you know, just as clear as the sun shines that you're saved from that place of ruin, that you're a Child of God and that, you know without a shadow of a doubt you belong to the Lord and are saved from that place of horrors. Don't put it off, don't wait too late men, women, boys and girls.

One night a preacher was preaching faithfully as I'm trying to preach to you and sitting back in the back was a girl about sixteen years of age in the church and the Pastor of the church went to her and said, as the invitation, was given, Margaret we've been praying for you, want you go tonight sometimes you'll want to accept Jesus. She looked at him and said preacher I'm not ready to give up the world, I'm not ready to accept Christ, I'm not ready to become a Christian and the preacher reasoned with her, he was trying to show her that she needed to be saved and come to Jesus now and she grew a bit angry and said, Preacher I'm not ready to give up the world,

I'm not ready to accept Christ, I'm not ready to become a Christian and finally she stomped out into the night in a huff and angry at the pastor. She went home and retired but God was troubling her, she couldn't sleep and finally she just said to God, God please take this burden away I'm not ready to give up the world, I'm not ready to accept Christ, I'm not ready to become a Christian, please take this burden away and God removed the burden. Listen to me, my friends, there are people all over Flint, Michigan tonight who'll sleep like babies, but who'll soon be in hell. That girl slept that night but the next morning when who awoke she wasn't feeling very well. Her loved ones made her stay in bed. Late in the afternoon they had to call the doctor. Three days later she was dying. That doctor walked in the daddy's room and said your little girl is dying shall I tell her or will you tell her, and that daddy with a sad heart said I'll tell her. He walked in the room, she saw it on his face. She said Daddy what time is it. He told her. She said I'll soon be in a place where there won't be any time, Daddy bring me some water. He brought her some water. She said I'll soon be in a place where there won't be any water. Then she screamed out, Daddy hold me up my feet are slipping into the fire and she fell back into his arms dead and her soul slipped into hell where she is lost and lost forever. Let every head be bowed please tonight and every eye closed.

Precious Memories

"Most God called preachers attempt to practice what they preach. More than any man I have ever known Jesse Hendley could have glorified the Lord if he had chosen to preach what he practiced. He was consumed with an uncompromising love for Jesus Christ; and his sermons were delivered from the overflow of his intimacy with his blessed Savior. His perspective on eternity stood in sharp contrast to most mortals' preoccupation with this present world."

J. Gerald Harris, editor, The Christian Index

In the studio of WMAZ with Jimmy Waters.

GOD'S LAST CALL
Proverbs 1:24-29

Let us bow our heads, friends, in just a word of holy prayer as we go into God's Word again tonight. "Our father, we thank You tonight for this privilege one more time of standing as a dying man before dying men, women, boys and girls with the Gospel of Christ and the Word of God. We know Lord, that during these days we have been together hearts have been moved. I thank You for those who have made decisions for Christ. We thank You for every soul that has been saved, every soul that has opened its heart to the Savior, everyone who has made a rededication to God, everyone that has been drawn back to the Bible and back to prayer, back to witnessing, back to putting God, Christ and His Kingdom and righteousness first and the work of our blessed Lord first in our lives. We are conscious, Lord, that in spite of the blessings for which we do praise Thee, and for those who have labored for which we are grateful, there are always those who have been moved but have not yielded, have stifled the voice of conviction, the voice of God's Spirit, the voice of God's Word, and have been running from God. Our Father, we pray tonight that You show us the folly of such procedure. May this be the hour when people answer God's call, before it is too late. For we ask it, our Father, in Jesus' name and for His sake alone. Amen."

I want to speak to you tonight on "GOD'S LAST CALL," and I want to read to you from the first chapter of the Book of Proverbs, verses 24 through 29. God's Word says, Because I have called and ye refused; I have stretched out My hand and no man regarded; but ye have set at naught all My counsel, and would none of My reproof: I also will laugh at your calamity; I will mock when your fear cometh; when your fear cometh as desolation and your destruction cometh as a whirlwind; when distress and anguish cometh upon you. Then shall they call upon Me but I will not answer; they shall seek Me early, but they shall not find Me for that they hated knowledge: and did not choose the fear of the Lord."

Those are very terrible words, my friends. God's outstretched hand---that's His invitation---rejected. God's counsel---that's His word of direction---refused. God's reproof---against sin---unheeded. God Almighty, says these very terrible words: "I will laugh at your calamity. I will mock when your fear cometh." You say, "I don't understand that, Preacher." Neither do I. Neither do I. You say, "You preached the other night on THE LOVE of God." I certainly did. But there is THE WRATH of God in the Bible, too, besides the love of God. The folly of this present hour is that people will lift out of the Bible certain truths and not balance them with other truths found in God's Word. I want to say to you tonight, friends, that that's the surest way that I know for us to be lost.

Now my subject is "God's Last Call," and my text is Proverbs 1:24-28. God says, "Because I have called and you refused, you will call upon Me but I will not answer." Your destruction is coming. Your whirlwind, sickness and death, is coming upon you. Then you will call upon Me, but I will not answer. You will seek Me early, but you will not find Me, because you hated knowledge and did not choose the fear of the Lord." Now I want to remind you tonight, my friend, that you do not need more sermons. You need to make a decision. You need to get into the ark of safety.

When D. L. Moody was preaching in the city of Chicago one summer, he preached five successive nights on the Lord Jesus, taking various truths from Jesus' life. On that fifth night he took that famous text of Pilate's, "What shall I do then with Jesus which is called Christ?" And he pressed upon that audience the fact that that is a question facing every human soul in the world, and the GREATEST question that faces each one of us. "What am I going to do with Jesus? What am I going to do with Jesus which is called Christ?"

When he got through with his message, came to the end of it, he said, "Now, friends, I am going to give you a week to make your decision, what you will do with Jesus. No invitation tonight. No invitation at all. I am not going to give you a chance to do it. I want you to go your way and think for one solid week what you want to do with Jesus, and come back a week from now and tell us what you want to do with Jesus which is called Christ." Moody never forgave himself for dismissing an audience without demanding their decision, for no sooner had he dismissed that audience than the Fire bells began to ring. The famous Chicago fire was on.

And Mr. Moody had reason to believe that there were people in that service that night who were burned to death in the path of the flames. Many of them doubt-less were unsaved. Moody said, Never again will I dismiss an audience without demanding that they make their decision for Christ." And he never did, after that time. Tonight, my friends, I demand that you make your decision for the Lord Jesus Christ.

The first thing we have in our text tonight, the first thing the Bible teaches, is that GOD CALLS MEN. God calls men. God is calling you. You say, "How does God call men?" First of all, God calls men by His providential dealings, His providences. I mean the everyday happenings that He sends your way, calculated to make you think about your soul and death and dying and your sins and Christ and salvation and getting right with God.

You remember that when John Wesley was a little lad the parish house caught on fire. A neighbor saw that the lad was not among those rescued. He looked toward the burning building and saw the boy behind a pane of glass and the flames licking up beside him, and the boy's face showed terror. He ran and grabbed a neighbor and climbed to his shoulder and broke the glass and reached up and rescued that little boy just in time to save him from a horrible death. John Wesley was just a little boy, but he never forgot that he had been saved from a terrible, roasting death. And he said, "God saved me for a purpose and I am going to devote my life to this God Who saved me from that burning death." And he did that very thing.

How many times, my friends, has some serious illness come your way, and you thought, "I might have died." Or you were in some near accident and you felt the cold chill of death on your spine and you thought, "I might have been killed. Where would I have been? God's providential dealings, trying to get you to repent, trying to get you to come to Christ. God calls by His providences, His providential dealings.

Then God calls by the Bible and Bible-loving Christians around about you. When Dr. I. M. Haldeman was pastor of the great First Baptist Church of New York City, there came walking down the aisle one night a New York businessman. He looked in the preacher's face and said, "Dr. Haldeman, tell me, will we know each other in heaven?"

Dr. Haldeman looked at him and said, "Why do you ask?" He said, "Well, I lived on a South Georgia farm when I was a boy, and I was the black sheep in the family. My mother was a godly woman. The only book she ever read, I suppose, was the Bible. She loved the Bible. She loved Christ. That's all she talked about---her religion, her Christ, and her Bible. And I got tired of it and I ran away from home and I came here to New York City. At first, I had it pretty rough. Then I began to make money hand over fist, I forgot that little godly mother on that South Georgia farm, until one day I received a telegram, "Better hurry home if you expect to see mother alive." I rushed there as quickly as I could get there, but I got there too late. She was dead. I walked into that little country parlor, and I bent over the dead face of my mother as I was alone in that room with her corpse and as I looked in her face all the remorse of the way I mistreated her began to sweep over my soul." This businessman looked in the preacher's face and he said, "Preacher, I'd give ten thousand dollars right now to look in the face of my mother again and tell her how sorry I am that I mistreated her." That man was saying that, that little godly mother was God's call to him to be a Christian. That little mother's Bible was God's call to Him to read of the Christ of the Bible and believe on the Bible and live the Bible and put his trust in his mother's Christ.

How many times have you seen a Bible that was God's call to you but you didn't believe it and live it. You've seen an earnest

Christian; you never ran into a real, genuine Christian yet that you didn't respect that Christian. You thought in your heart, "I ought to be a Christian like that. I ought to be a child of God like that." God calls by the Bible and Bible-loving Christians.

Then God calls by faithful preachers of the Word of God. I have been in this business a pretty long time now and know something about what people think about preachers. "I like this man's delivery." "I don't like this man's delivery." "I like this man's emphasis." "I don't like this man's emphasis." "I like this preacher's personality," "I don't like this preacher's personality." People catalogue preachers. Hear me, my friends. It doesn't matter about the preacher. It doesn't matter about his delivery. It doesn't matter about his emphasis, as long as he preaches the Word of God to you. It doesn't matter about his personality. It doesn't matter whether he is handsome or not. It doesn't matter whether he mouths pleasing words or not. The only thing that matters is the message. If it is God's message, and if that preacher preached to you the Word of God in love and grace and honesty and truth and sincerity, he was God's messenger to you.

Do you know why Israel has suffered these two thousand years like she has? God says in Second Chronicles 36, "They mocked the messengers of God and despised His Word and misused His prophets till wrath is risen and there is no remedy." We cannot mock the messengers of God. We cannot despise God's Word. We cannot misuse the preachers of God's Word, without bringing upon our heads the damnation of our souls. I don't say that because of man. I don't say that because I am a preacher. I am saying that it doesn't matter about the messenger if he is true to God. The important thing is the message.

If you have heard preachers who were God-called men, whether you liked their personalities or not, or their emphases, or their anything else, their deliveries, you have heard the Gospel. God has sent it to you. You are not a heathen in Africa. You are not living in India where they have never heard. You are not living in South America under the bondage of a false religion. You have sat under faithful preaching of the Word of God. You have heard not one, not two, not five or ten, not twenty or a hundred---you have heard the Gospel of the Son of God from God-called preachers again and again and again. And I want to say to you, every time you heard it, it was God's message to you that night, that day. It was God's call. God calls by faithful preachers of the Word of God.

Then the fourth call of God is a very grim one. When people won't listen any other way, God many times resorts to death. He may take out of your arms somebody you love better than your life, to make you repent if you won't repent any other way. I have seen Him do it again and again. God may have to take a baby out of your arms to bow your head and bend your knee and yield to the Lord Jesus.

One of the saddest funerals I ever had was in East Point cemetery a few years ago. It was the funeral service of a little tiny babe, one of those infant funeral services. On the way out to the cemetery I said, "Lord, give me something to say. I think He did. We stood around that pitiful little graveside, the tiny hole in the ground, the little casket, the little two-by-fours. There is something very pitiful about an infant's funeral service. I said, "This baby is better off than some of us around this graveside. This child never reached the age of accountability, it never heard about Jesus. It had never rejected the Savior. It never had the chance. When it died the Lord took care of it. That child is in heaven but some of us around this graveside may have rejected the Savior and be lost while this child is yonder in heaven." A man began to sob and move over toward his automobile. He was the daddy of the child. When I got through with my remarks and my prayer, I went over to him and put my arms around him and he was weeping up against his car. I said, "Old fellow, you want to meet your baby again." He said, "I sure do, Preacher." I said, "Let's pray." He dropped to his knees out there that Saturday afternoon in that sunshiny cemetery, and he wept his way to Jesus Christ. God had to take his baby out of his arms to make him think seriously, make him bend his knee and come to Jesus.

It may be a wife, my friends, God will take out of your arms if you won't repent any other way. I think sometimes that one of the saddest funerals I ever had was that of a twenty-eight-year-old mother at Autrey and Lowndes funeral home here in Atlanta. She had never accepted Christ until one day about six weeks before she died, as she was on her death bed, she heard one of my broadcasts.

A friend of mine told me that when I got to the end of the broadcast and gave the invitation to bow their heads and pray she prayed and asked God to save her for Christ's sake. She left her husband and two little boys. I walked into the chapel at the funeral home. Her body was in front of me. When my time came to speak, I rose to speak, I saw that husband sitting over here and those two little boys, one on either side of him. As I began to speak, the younger of those boys ran from his daddy's knee over to the casket. He would pat the casket and run back to his daddy's knees weeping, "I haven't got any mommy anymore!" All during that service that little boy would go to the casket where his dead mother's body was and would run back to his daddy's knees crying, "I haven't got my mommy anymore!" That little boy couldn't talk to you about death. He couldn't give you a dissertation about death. He didn't know anything about death, but he knew that his dead mother's body was in that casket and she wasn't coming home anymore, and his heart was broken. Every time that little boy would come back to his daddy's knees that man's head would drop a little bit lower until it was resting on his hands on his knees, as the blackness of hell came over his soul. He didn't have Christ. He had no Savior in the hours of death. If you don't think it pays to have Christ, go to the place of mourning! That's where the payoff comes! You go to a place where they have no Christ, and you've got midnight, blackness. You go to a place where they have Christ, and there is a victory over death.

They put her body in the hearse and went out yonder to the cemetery. We went up the side of the hill, they put the casket down on a mechanical device. I stood at the head of it. That man sat down with those little kids. As the body of that precious wife was being lowered into that cold grave, that man couldn't stand it any longer. With a sob he tore himself from that graveside and slipped to the back seat of his automobile, these motherless children behind him, and I was right behind them. I said, "Old fellow, you want to be saved, and raise these children for Jesus, and meet her again?" he said, "I do, Preacher!" I said, "Let's pray," and that man scrambled down on the back seat of his automobile and wept his way to Jesus Christ. He will tell you, "God had to take my wife out of my arms to make me repent. I wouldn't listen any other way."

It may be a daddy or a mother that you love with all your soul that God will have to take Home to make you repent. Sam Jones, the famous Cartersville evangelist, was a drunkard. He had been drunk for six weeks when he came stumbling in. The old daddy saw his son swaying at the foot of the bed. Being a Christian daddy, he began to sob out, "My poor wayward boy! You've broken your wife's heart and you've brought me down to an early grave." And the old man began to choke up, and under those scathing, burning words Jones, half-drunk, stumbled out of the room. Later when his daddy died, before the undertaker came for the body, now sobered up, he slipped back into that room and locked the door and he got down beside the corpse of his daddy and he said, "O Jesus, if You can save a wretch like me, save me right now!" And Jesus Christ came into Sam Jones' heart and transformed him instantly and called him to preach, and he became one of the greatest evangelists we have ever had in the world.

Many a time Sam Jones shook giant audiences when he said, "My friends, God had to put the corpse of my daddy across my pathway to turn me back from hell to heaven." It took his daddy's life to make him repent of his sins. God calls men, when they won't listen in any other way---to save them from eternal doom, many times by removing a loved one by death. God calls men.

God calls men, then there comes THE LAST CALL. "Because I have called and you refused, now you call for Me but I will not answer." A LAST CALL? Oh, yes, there comes the last call. You say, "What happens then when a man hears God's last call and turns it down?" God gives him up! We read in the Book of Hosea, "Ephraim is joined to his idols; let him alone." "Let him alone, Preacher. Don't ever preach a sermon that will reach that man. Wife, never pray a prayer that will ever reach the Throne of Grace. Let him alone, Holy Spirit: Don't ever convict him anymore. I'm through with him. Let him go on to hell, no more stops, no more bothers. Let him go. I'm done. I'm through. Henceforth there is just an inch between him and hell, which waits for him and where he will be with other reprobates.

To be sure, He may flourish a little while, like Saul after his rejection, or like the Pharisees in Jesus' day. You may go to church twenty more years but you'll never, never, never be moved by God's Spirit like you were that night you turned Him down! Never again will you be MOVED enough to move for God and Christ! You never will.

Then Ezekiel's terrible word will be fulfilled: "Destruction cometh, and you will seek peace, and there will be none." You say, "Well, I'll get somebody to pray for me." May I remind you that the prayers of loved ones and friends will not avail for you when GOD gives you up. Who can pray for a man or woman or boy or girl whom the God of Heaven has GIVEN UP? Who can REACH God for somebody that GOD has given up? The One who opens and shuts the gate. HE is the one who determines who is going in and who is going to be shut out. Prayers of ministers, loved ones and friends will not avail.

God reproved Samuel for praying for Saul. Shut up, Samuel. Don't talk to Me about Saul anymore. I have given him up. Jeremiah, praying for the Jews; Shut up, Jeremiah. Don't talk to Me anymore. I've given them up. Nothing will avail.

You remember what happened back yonder when Samaria was being besieged by the enemy and the people were starving to death. One morning a poor, starving woman was walking on the street and she saw the king on the wall, and she sobbed out, O king, give us bread! You know what he said? He said, "Woman, if THE LORD help thee not, whence shall I help thee? If God holds back the bread, what can a king do?"

75

I am asking you, If the God of Heaven shuts the gate of heaven to your soul, who can do anything for you? Prayers will not avail when God gives you up. When that last call comes and you refuse it, God gives you up. "Ephraim is joined to his idols; let him alone." Then what?

When God gives you up, HELL IS INEVITABLE. Let me say again, you may live a little longer. You may go to church. You may go through religious motions. But the Spirit of God has long departed. You cannot be saved without God's SPIRIT! "Except a man be born of the Spirit of God, he cannot enter the Kingdom of God." When the Spirit departs, there is no hope for a man's soul. That is what happens when you turn down God's last call. Hell is inevitable.

Have you ever considered the first five minutes after death? I have often thought about it. The greatest Adventure you and I will ever make will be the first five minutes after death. Just think of it. I have often thought of it myself. I am going to see the Face of God, the first minutes after death. The face of Jesus! I am going to see the face of my mother and the face of my dad and loved ones and friends and converts who have gone on to heaven. Oh, that tremendous adventure! The first five minutes when GLORY breaks on the face of a child of God! What a tremendous moment it is going to be, a tremendous time.

Have you ever considered what the first five minutes after death will be for the unsaved? May I suggest that the first minute after death you will lift up your eyes in a new place. It will be hell; it won't be heaven. A woman was in the hospital. Like many people she had forgotten to look after her soul--- everything else but her soul. The doctor walked in and told her she was going to die. She had never realized it. She came face to face with the fact for the first time. It shocked her, and she fell out of that bed screaming, "have mercy on me!" and dropped dead right on the spot. She lifted up the eyes of her soul in hell.

There are only two places in eternity. If it is not going to be heaven, it will be hell. The first minute after death for the unsaved, they will lift up their eyes IN HELL! What an awful thing it must be to find one's self in a hell you never planned to go to, but you didn't do anything about, to keep out of it. The second minute after death, may I suggest, you will realize your new master. It won't be Jesus; it will be the devil. There are only two masters in eternity. I have tried to tell you, when that heart stops beating you will either be looking into the Face of Jesus or you will be looking into the face of the devil. One of them will be your master for eternity! That is the Scriptures. I don't want to meet the devil and his crowd. I don't want to spend my eternity with the devil and his crowd. I want to be with JESUS! But, the unsaved, you will realize that your new master will be the devil, who has brought every heartache and sorrow and tear the human family has ever known. You will sorrow throughout the ages of eternity!

The third minute after death, your new companions. They won't be the best people in the world; they will be the worst. You don't have to invite to your home tonight drunkards and harlots and dope fiends and sex perverts and liars and thieves and gamblers and kidnappers. You don't have to associate with the vilest people in the world, but that is going to be your crowd in the next world.

God lumps up all the unsaved in the same lump. "The fearful, the unbelieving, the abominable, the whoremongers, sorcerers, idolaters, all liars, shall have their share in the lake of fire that burneth with brimstone which is the second death."

There is the word FEARFUL. It means cowards; people who are cowards will not take their stand for Jesus. They are afraid somebody will laugh at them, afraid what the business world says, afraid what the social world says, afraid they can't make enough money, afraid of this and afraid of that. Beloved friends, what does a man CARE when the world is on fire, about man, if he is right with GOD? It doesn't matter about man.

Then the word UNBELIEVER. An unbeliever! That is the best woman in this city, and the best man in this city, OUT OF CHRIST, who haven't believed on Jesus with their whole heart in faith and belief that SAVES them, leading them to join the church and be baptized and live a godly, holy life. They are going to spend eternity with the vilest people the world has ever known. They are the words of God; they are not my words. I didn't write the Bible.

Then may I suggest, the fourth minute after death you will realize your new, fixed heart and character. Will you listen to me one moment? If nothing has made you think, will you listen to this, please? Unsaved in that lost world, your character will be one FIXED IN SIN FOREVER. You can never be any better. You will grow worse through the ages of eternity. At the close of the Bible God says, "He that is unrighteous, let him be unrighteous still. He that is filthy, let him be filthy still. He that is holy, let him be holy still. he that is righteous, let him be righteous still." What does God say? What you are when you come to die is what you will be forever. If you die saved, you will be a holy man in heaven forever. If you die unsaved, you will be a sinner forever, and there is no redemption for sin.

There is no regeneration, there is no blood that cleanses. You will be a sinner forever. You will never be a better man or woman. You will grow rotten and worse through the ages of eternity. The drunkard will have his passion for drink unsatisfied. The lustful, lecherous man will have his passions unsatisfied. The liar, the thief, the man who worshipped gold and was covetous, instead of his God, will lust for these things in the next world still, because he has an unregenerate heart and an unregenerate life. They had never let GOD come into their hearts.

Then may I suggest, the fifth minute after death you will realize your new condition. Will you hear me now? I want to say very carefully, JESUS SAYS it will be one of intense agony and pain, weeping and wailing and gnashing of teeth. They are His own words. An infidel came one night to hear a preacher preach as I am trying to preach to you. He professed not to believe in the Bible, God, heaven, hell, in anything at all spiritual that we hold very precious. He walked out of that meeting with the Word of God ringing in his heart and in his mind.

A man can say he doesn't believe, but he has got to face God's Word, and he knows in his heart that this Bible IS God's Word. All the way home he couldn't rest. He was disturbed. Three days later, and no sleep, he rushed back to the preacher. He said, "Preacher. I am distressed. I have ridiculed Jesus. I have denied God's existence. I have picked flaws in His Word. I have cursed my Maker. I am lost!

The preacher said, "Do you want us to pray for you?" He said, "It won't do any good. I am doomed and I deserve it." Within three months time he pined away, a poor lost soul.

Oh, the first five minutes after death for that poor, lost man or woman outside of Christ! God's Word speaks of hell as a prison, a lake of fire, a devouring fire, a place of everlasting burnings, a furnace of fire, a place of torment, a place of eternal pun-ishment, a place where you'll never rest, a place where your breath is a living flame, a place where you will drink of the wine of the wrath of Gad, a place where you will be tormented day and night forever and ever, a place where you will not want your loved ones to come, a place where you will spend eternity with the devil and his angels, a place where you will be with murderers, liars and thieves, a place where the smoke of your torment will ascend up forever and ever!

You will recognize that every one of these utterances I have lifted right out of the pages of the Bible, GOD'S HOLY WORD.

In the light of what I have said to you, and it is TRUE, there are three observations I want to make. To the young people who are here tonight, let me suggest that you not expect to be saved beyond your youth. It is a matter of record, and I have tried to tell audiences up and down the land---it is a matter of psychology and human nature that eighty percent of the people who are saved are saved between eight and sixteen years of age. Beyond sixteen, it plummets to fifteen percent of the people. Most people who get beyond sixteen never come to Christ. The ages between eight and sixteen years should settle the question about whether you are going to be a Christian or not, whether you are going to heaven or not, whether you will take Christ and live an honest-to-goodness Christian life or not.

Yonder was a girl sixteen years of age from a very wealthy family. They gave her culture. They gave her clothes. They gave her travel. They gave her cars. They gave her friends, they gave her parties---everything a girl's heart could desire. Except one thing: GOD. They didn't know God. They couldn't give her GOD. At sixteen years of age this girl came down to death's door, and as the darkness of death was crowding in, terror gripped the heart of that precious girl, as it will the heart of every unsaved person when they come to the end of the way. She sobbed out, "Daddy! Mamma! Come! Go with me! It's getting dark." But all they could say was, "Honey, this is one trip we can't take with you. We could go all over Europe with you, and we could cross the seas and everywhere else, but we can't make the trip of death with you." She was lost. She sobbed out, "Daddy! Mamma! Pray for me. I'm lost!" Well, they didn't know how to pray---poor, godless parents in the hour when their child was DYING, UNSAVED. Can't pray! Do not know God! While the daddy went to get the preacher to come and pray for his dying girl, she DIED.... and went to hell. She had lived sixteen years but didn't look after the most important thing in the world, the salvation of her soul, the acceptance of Jesus. Do not expect to be saved beyond your youth, young people. Make ready to meet God, as God says, "Remember now thy Creator in the days of thy youth."

You older folk, do not expect for a single moment that you will have a more tender heart toward Christ and God. You never will have. You are not getting any tenderer; you are getting harder as the days go by. It is the truth of God's Word.

D. L. Moody went into a certain city for a revival meeting, went into the hotel, and the man behind the desk extended his hand and said, "Mr. Moody, I believe." Moody said, as he shook his hand, "Brother you have the best of me. I don't think I remember you." Then he said, "You remember such-and-such a meeting, the closing night?" "Oh," he said, "Yes, you are the man who told me you were going home and make your decision about accepting Christ. What did you do?" He said, "I did just what I told you I would do, Mr. Moody. I went home and made my decision. I went home and sat down at a desk and got a pencil and piece of paper and I drew a line down the middle of that paper and I put on one side what I would gain in this world's goods by rejecting Christ, and what I would gain by accepting Christ. What I would lose of the things of this world by rejecting Christ, and what I would lose if I accepted Jesus. I weighed the matter and Mr. Moody, I decided to TAKE THE WORLD and GIVE UP JESUS CHRIST." Moody said it looked like a demon itself came on his face as he cried out, "Mr. Moody, since that day I have HATED the Name of Jesus Christ!" Moody said tears washed down his cheeks to think that a man's SOUL, that was once tender, as a boy, could ever get so HARD that he would hate the Name of the Blessed One Who yonder on the bloody cross died for his sins, TO SAVE him, that he might be SAVED.

You are not getting any tenderer, God's Word warns, "Lest you be HARDENED by the deceitfulness of sin." That is why older folks don't come to Christ. That's why it is easier for younger people to come. Old man SIN has hardened hearts! The world, the flesh and the devil have been around to grip the soul. When a man or woman is lost, it is so hard to tear loose and come! My last word is, do not any of you friends in this room ever expect to have another chance to be saved! THIS is your chance, right now. Did you ever consider that passage where God says, and He is talking to you, "Behold, Behold, NOW is the accepted time. TODAY is the day of salvation." What does He mean? He means that NOW is the only time you've got to be saved. "Oh," you say, I'll be saved yesterday." No, you won't. "Last week. Last month. Ten years ago." You can't be saved in the PAST; it is gone. You can't give your heart to Jesus in the past; it is gone, irrevocably gone. You say, "I'll be saved TOMORROW." Show me where God guarantees you another hour to live! The only time that you absolutely can count on to be saved is RIGHT Now. That is the only time. And that is the meaning of that passage. Any intelligent person will agree with God. Now is the accepted time. THIS is the time God has given you to be saved.NOW! And the biggest thing that faces me is the salvation of my precious SOUL and my relationship with my GOD and the relationship of my wife and my children and my family with my God.

I want to tell you of two man who heard God's Last Call through my voice. One of them grabbed it and now is in heaven; the other rejected it and now is in hell. I was preaching right here in this city a few years ago, closing a meeting. For years I have closed a meeting with this message on God's Last Call. When I got through (it was raining that day) three men walked down the aisle. One stood before that audience and lifted nearly every one of us out of our seats. He said, "My friends, I feel like that preacher is talking about me, and this is my last call. I have turned down God so long. I have hardened my heart so long. I should have been saved when I was young but I didn't. I am not young anymore. I have gotten harder with the days and the year. God has spoken, and His voice is getting quieter and quieter and the pull is getting less and less. He said, "I believe this is my LAST CALL, and I am going on record publicly and before God and Christ and angels and man as accepting Jesus Christ as my SAVIOR."

I went on about my business. A preacher called me a few days later and said, "Do you remember that experience?" I said, "Yes." He said, he was drowned in Chesapeake Bay the other day. They fished his body out. They are sending it back for the funeral. I want you to come and help me in the funeral service." You can imagine how we felt when they brought his body right back in the same spot where just a few days before I had preached to him on God's Last Call, and he walked down the aisle and grabbed the chance, saying, "I feel this is God's last call for me." He was saved. He answered the call of God! It was God's last call, under my voice, to him THAT NIGHT.

Let me tell you of another man. I was preaching in Newnan, Georgia, closing a tent meeting with "God's Last Call." Sitting out in that audience Was a man, beside him his precious wife. She was an earnest Christian. He hadn't yet accepted Jesus. All during that week we had been praying for him, loved ones and friends and other Christians. That night as I preached, the last chance, she stood by and she grabbed his arm. She cried. She prayed. I gave the invitation. She looked up in his face, tears rolling down her cheeks, begging her husband to come and accept the Saviour and be saved and come to heaven with her. You could see him harden himself. You could see him grip his chair. You could see him fight off the Spirit of God. You could almost feel the Spirit of God lift him and hurl him forward, but he would pull back and say NO to the Spirit of GOD!

The revival meeting ended. He walked out that night unsaved. At three o'clock in the morning we were aroused from our slumber with the voice of that precious young wife; "My husband was electrocuted on the job just a few minutes ago!"

That man had walked OUT of that meeting where I had preached on God's Last Call. About ten o'clock he went home and got a bite to eat, went to his work at midnight, and on the job at three in the morning he was ELECTROCUTED. Five hours after he had heard me preach on God's last call, God called him into eternity. He was lost forever! It was GOD'S LAST CALL, under my poor voice that night!

Let every head be bowed, please, and every eye closed. "Our Father! Thou dost know every beating heart in this room. Lord, we have come with Your Word, one more time. Now is the accepted time. Today is the day of salvation. Because I have called, and ye refused, you will call upon Me but I will not answer. You will seek Me early, but you will not find Me, for that you hated knowledge and did not choose the fear of the Lord. O God, tonight, if this is the last call for somebody in this room under our poor voice, may they head the Messenger of Life this moment, for the Messenger of Death is waiting if somebody turns down the call tonight, the Call of God! The Invitation to eternal life, salvation, heaven! God, help men and women, boys and girls, answer the Call of God tonight, TO DO what God is CALLING them to do. For we ask it in Jesus' name and for His sake.   Amen."

We are going to stand and sing the invitation song. God is calling you TONIGHT. If you do not know you are saved, slip out of your seat and come. If you are an unenlisted, unaffiliated Baptist, God is calling you to come and move that letter. If you need to rededicate your life, God is calling you to rededication. If you need to surrender to the Lord, if you do not know you are saved, as certainly as the sun shone today GOD IS CALLING YOU TONIGHT to salvation and eternal life. While we sing, will you slip out of your seat and come. Come right on, while God is speaking!

"Just as I am, without one plea..." Slip right out of your sent and come tonight. The Lord bless you! Do what God is calling you to do tonight. The Lord bless you! Husbands and wives, come on, TONIGHT. Sons and daughters, young people, come TONIGHT. DO what God is CALLING you to do. If you do not know you are saved, come. If God is calling you to rededicate your life, come TONIGHT, while God is speaking to your heart. Just a moment, please. Heads bowed and eyes closed. How many of you friends in this room know that GOD HAS SPOKEN tonight? HIS WORD is what I am talking about, and HIS SPIRIT, not my voice. I am not anybody; I am just a messenger boy. The preacher doesn't matter; all that matters is GOD and YOUR SOUL and the HOLY SPIRIT and HIS WORD and what you will do about it.

While heads are bowed and eyes are closed, how many of you can say tonight, "Brother Hendley, I know beyond a shadow of a doubt that I am saved, that if I died tonight, I know I will be in heaven with Jesus; will you raise your hand? You'll be honest about it. All right, please lower your hands. "Here and there over the audience, are dear friends who cannot say, "I know I am saved." God is calling you tonight. God is calling you to know it. You will know it when you are saved. Jesus said, "He that follows Me shall not walk in darkness but shall have the light of life." When you are saved you will not be in the dark about it; you will know it. If you don't know it, you are lost, because when you are saved GOD comes into your heart and you will KNOW it. It is impossible for GOD to come in and you not know it.

Listen, He is calling you tonight. Mothers, what about your children? How would you feel if your child died tonight without Christ? Husband, how would you feel about your wife if she died without Christ? Your loved ones? Your friends? GOD IS SPEAKING. This may be the last call for some man or woman, for some boy or girl. GOD IS SPEAKING TO YOU. Come on, while he is speaking, and answer the Call. Whatever God is telling you to do, do it, while we sing softly. Pray Christian, with all your might. Turn to your friends or loved ones and invite them to come with you. God, bless you. Don't be afraid. Just step out for Jesus. I'd be afraid NOT TO. Don't be afraid to come to Him. I'd be afraid to go away without Him. NOW IS THE ACCEPTED TIME.

God bless these precious souls! Keep praying, Christians. If you are a Christian, a child of God, hold on in earnest prayer for lost friends and loved ones. Some of you husbands and wives ought to walk down this aisle and promise God you will have a family altar and raise these children around the Bible and prayer. Husbands, why don't you take your God-given office as high priest in your home, for God says YOU are to bring up your children in the nurture and admonition of the Lord, not the wife or Sunday School teacher or the preacher or evangelist.

The husbands and fathers are to bring up the children in the nurture and admonition of the Lord! Have you led your children to Christ? Do you pray with them? Do you read them the Bible, the Word of God? Do you teach them, as God says? Will you take them to God's House and set an example of spirituality before them? Come on tonight and do what God is telling you to do: that it may be well with you.

Are you an unaffiliated Baptist, and your church letter is somewhere else while you live in this community? God is calling you to get into a good, warm church where you can serve Him with honesty and sincerity and truth. You can't do it with a divided membership or by coming occasionally....(All of this appeal was over music, "Just As I am.")

Precious Memories

"Dr. Jesse Hendley was one of those rare men of God who lived out the combination of personal integrity, intellectual depth, Biblical wisdom, powerful oratory and above all the always fresh anointing of the Holy Spirit. In short, he was a fearless man of God.

As a pastor for 36 years, I led my church in at least two revivals, conferences, or evangelistic campaigns every year. It was our blessing to use Jesse Hendley on several occasions. He never failed to bless our church and help us have a harvest of souls.

Two memories are very vivid and help to sum up the heart of this dear man.

I was pastor of the First Baptist Church of Kenner, LA, a New Orleans suburb for 13 years. I was invited by one of the prominent professors at New Orleans to teach one session of his class on the Book of Revelation. He had taught the entire term from the Preterist or Historical perspective of eschatology. He invited me to come for one session to share the pre-millennial, pre-tribulation, dispensational viewpoint. So I was to have 50 minutes to share that perspective. I agreed to come but then I discovered the date he wanted was when Jesse was to be with us for a conference. I asked the professor if Dr. Hendley could take my place. He replied, "I just want someone who holds to that eschatological view to share it with the students." And did he ever! Jesse Hendley overcame an entire term of erroneous teaching in just 50 minutes. I honestly believe those seminary students were convinced of true doctrine that day and have taught from that perspective to this very day.

Another vivid memory was a phone call I received from Jesse when he was very late in his life. He had been invited to a church for a meeting and this is what he asked. I can hear his raspy voice to this very moment. 'Ron, Ron you know this church, do they really want revival? I have only a small amount of time left and my energy is almost gone. Are they serious about having revival? I don't want to come if they are not serious.

To be honored to write these memories about a great man of God has allowed me to reflect and cry out to God, do it again, Lord, do it again."

Ron Herrod
R.H.E.M.A. International

Though the picture is hard to make out,
Brother Jesse is to the far left dealing with a man's soul.

THE WORLD CRISIS AND THE ONLY WAY OUT

HEAVEN – WILL WE KNOW EACH OTHER?
Matthew 8:11-12

Tonight I want to speak to you on the subject, Heaven, and will we know each other there. Our Lord's Word in Matthew 8:11,12 Jesus says, "And I say unto you, that many shall come from the east and west, and shall sit down with Abraham, and Isaac and Jacob, in the kingdom of heaven. But the children of the kingdom shall be cast out into outer darkness: there shall be weeping and gnashing of teeth."

Let me remind you these are the words of the Lord. He says, "I say unto you." If there is an authority on heaven that authority of course will be the Lord Jesus Christ. We want to hear what He has to say tonight about heaven. The first thing we learn is there is going to be a lot of people in heaven. Jesus says, many shall come. I'm glad there are going to be a lot of people in heaven. Billy Sunday used to say, don't let God hang a "For Rent" sign on your mansion in heaven. That's a very clever remark the only trouble about it is it just isn't so. There are not going to be any for rent signs on any mansions in heaven. There are not going to be any empty mansions yonder in heaven. God's commandment to His servants is to go into the highways and hedges and compel them to come in that my house may be filled.

The Gospel will continue to be preached and people will continue to believe until that complement of people who are to be in heaven shall be saved. Now, to be sure there are going to be more people in hell than there are going to be in heaven. If I were to be able to sit down and reason with you about heaven and hell and I ask you, do you think in the final analysis there will be more people wind up in heaven; only one person out of every million are genuinely saved. I don't know where he got his statistics but when I read that I said I certainly want to be one out of my million. I want to be in heaven. I don't want to miss heaven at all.

Charles Spurgeon, one of the greatest minds we have ever had as well as one of the greatest preachers used to reason like this, he said, Jesus would never let the devil beat Him out so Jesus will be able to win more people to heaven than the devil will be able to tempt to hell. The only trouble about that is that is human reasoning and what we want is the Word of God. Is there a statement in the Bible that indicates whether there are going to be more people in heaven or hell in the great final wind-up? I believe that there is. In the Sermon on the Mount, Jesus said, "Enter ye in at the straight gate: for wide is the gate, and broad is the way, that leads to destruction, and many there be which go in thereat: But straight is the gate, and narrow is the way, which leadeth unto life, and few, (F E W) there be that find it." Jesus said, it's many traveling the broad road to hell and it's few that find and travel the straight and narrow way to heaven. Now statistics bear that out.

Yonder in my home city in Atlanta, Georgia, a well churched city, 62% of the people never darken anybody's church door. Now of the other 48% of the people who do go to church, profess some religion. There are those who have no faith in Jesus Christ and of course they are not going to be saved for people without faith in Jesus will not be saved. Then out of the evangelical churches where Jesus is preached and taught and people believe we know that by no means will everybody be saved. There are those who will reject Christ. There are those whose hearts have not been touched. There are those who haven't been born again and they will be lost. I very much doubt that one fourth of the city of Atlanta is saved today. So we find statistics bearing out the Word of Jesus that it is many traveling the broad road to hell and it is few that travel the straight and narrow way that leads to life.

Now the next question that comes to us is, where are they coming from. There are going to be a lot of people in heaven. Many shall come. Where are they coming from? The answer is, Jesus says, they are coming from the east and west. That means from all over the entire world people will be coming in. At the great Baptist World alliance yonder in Atlanta, Georgia I remember when Dr. Truett stood and called that great assembly to order and they began to sing that great song, "All Hail the Power of Jesus Name, Let Angels Prostrate fall, bring forth the Royal Diadem and crown Him Lord of all." A shiver went over me from the top of my head to the bottom of my feet as I thought, that's the way it is going to be yonder in heaven when they are coming in from all over the east and west and sit down with Abraham, Isaac and Jacob in the Kingdom of God and sing the praises of the Lamb.

There were people at the Baptist World Alliance from every nation under the sun, the black man, the red, the yellow man, the white man. Every nation was represented except Red Russia. She had no representative. That's the way it is going to be in heaven. People are coming from all over the entire earth and there meet the Lord Jesus and their loved ones in that wonderful place.

Now the next thing that comes to us from the text tonight is this question, What are we going to do there? According to the text we are going to sit down with Abraham and Isaac and Jacob. Now the word for sit down is the Greek Word, anaklino, which means literally to recline at a feast with the emphasis on feasting. So they are going to feast yonder in heaven when we get there with the Lord. Heaven is a place of glorious, wonderful feasting.

Now some people say, you believe in heaven don't you preacher? I certainly do. I believe in heaven without a shadow of a doubt. I know that there is a heaven. You say, how do you know that there is a heaven? I know there is a heaven first of all because the Bible says so. The Bible says, Jesus said, "Lay not up for yourselves treasures on earth, but lay for yourselves treasures in heaven where moth and rust doth not corrupt, and where thieves do not break through and steal." We are to lay up our treasures in heaven not here on earth. Our Lord Jesus Christ said, when you pray say, Our Father, which art in heaven.

When you and I go to our prayer rooms we are not wasting time, we are not going through a spiritual exercise. We are talking to our Father yonder in heaven. We read, the Lord Jesus for these two thousand years has been in heaven. He has gone into heaven there to appear in the presence of God for us. Heaven has got to be a real place because there is a real man in a literal body in a literal place. Flint is a place. Atlanta, Georgia is a place. Hell is a place and heaven is a place. When He rose from the dead they thought He was a spirit. But spirits hath not flesh and bones as you see me have. So there is a real man and real place called heaven, the Lord Jesus and He has been there these two thousand years as He went up from the Mt. of Olives down here in this world.

Then the Apostle Paul in a tremendous spiritual experience tells us of being caught up into heaven. He said, I don't know whether I was in the body or out of the body but was caught up into heaven, into paradise and heard things unlawful for a man to utter. And because of the abundance of the revelation, he said God gave him a thorn in the flesh, a messenger from Satan to buffet him lest he be exalted over much. I believe what Paul wrote and I believe he walked the streets of gold and when he came back down here, God shut his lips and wouldn't let him tell us of the wonders that he saw because God knows we wouldn't be worth anything at all if we knew all the wonders of heaven. He told us all we need to know but he hasn't told us all we would like to know about that wonderful place.

Then anyone who is serious thinking about heaven will read very much the Book of the Revelation. You remember John the great Apostle of love who leaned on Jesus' breast was given the glorious privilege of writing one of the greatest books of all time, the book of the wind-up, the Book of Revelation. John was on the isle of Patmos with the Word of God and the testimony of Jesus and he said, "I became in spirit on the Lord's day" in which he was rapt into the spiritual world. He said, a door was opened in heaven and he heard a voice saying come up here and he said, immediately I was in the spirit. John tries to describe unto us what he saw in heaven.

He tries to describe the indescribable God sitting upon His rainbow encircled throne. He tells about the twenty-four thrones with the twenty-four elders. He tells us of the seven lamps of fire which are the seven spirits of God burning before the throne of God. He talks about those four living creatures, those strange super earthly creatures that wait upon God, crying, Holy, Holy, Holy is the Lord God Almighty day and night. He sees Jesus in the very midst of the throne as a Lamb having been slain which means with a mark of the crucifixion on His body for God is never going to let us forget what it cost Jesus Christ to save our souls. For the ages of eternity, He will bear on His face, on His hands, on His side and on His feet the marks of the crucifixion and billions of years from now we will never forget what the Lord Jesus Christ did for us. John sees Him as the Lamb in the midst of the throne.

Then he begins to hear the angels sing and he estimates there are between two hundred million and three hundred million of those super earthly beings that wait upon God day and night called the angels of God. They sing the praises of God and the Lamb in that happy world. Then he sees a great multitude which no man can number, of redeemed souls that were once sinners on earth, people as you and I but there they are in heaven. What a hope that is for us, if they can get there we can get there too. There they are clad in their white robes of absolute purity and holding in their hands palm branches representing festivity.

Where did they come from and back came the answer, these came out of the great tribulation and washed their robes and made them white in the blood of the Lamb, therefore are they before the throne of God and serving day and night in His temple and the Lamb which is in the midst of the throne shall lead them unto fountains of living water and God shall wipe away all tears from their eyes.

The Book of the Revelation is filled with wonderful truths about heaven. I believe there is a heaven first of all because the Bible says so. Then I believe there is a heaven because I desire one. Do you think maybe that's strange reasoning? It isn't so strange. Have you ever noticed that God has a compensation for every human desire? If you are hungry, God has provided food. If you are thirsty God has provided drink. If you need love God has provided these to love you. Shall He not provide for that greatest of all desires, for immortality? Nobody wants to die. Everybody wants to live, that is normal in any way whatsoever. So God will fulfill that desire.

Then there is a third reason why I know there is a heaven without a shadow of a doubt and that is because I have stood by so many death beds as saints of God would die. As they approached the very border line of this world and the next they saw something of the other world on the other side and whispered back something of the glory they saw and it was on their lips and on their face as they passed on into the next world.

I think of the man who ordained me to the ministry. One of the holiest preachers I ever knew died at 60 years of age in the Georgia Baptist Hospital in Atlanta. He called for me before he died and I went down to see him, he was whispering in his weakness approaching the shadow of the valley of death. I put my ear down close to his lips and he said, I saw a vision last night. I said, "What did you see man of God?" He said, "I saw a great white church with throngs and throngs of people." There was on his face a smile that isn't seen in this world believe me as he was thinking in anticipation of joining that happy crowd over on the other side. In just a matter of a few hours he was gone from this world and believe me there were no shadows when he died. There was no dark valley when Jesus came for his soul. He went to be with his Lord. It was a wonderful experience. Don't tell me that man hadn't gotten a glimpse of the other world.

I had a lady yonder in my church who died of cancer. While she was dying she would go into a coma and be talking to loved ones on the other side. She would brighten up and be talking to us. In one of her brighter moments she said, "Brother Hendley, I want you to pray for Jim." Jim was her husband. I turned round and I said, "Jim, what does she mean?" He said, "she is not rational preacher, she doesn't know what she is talking about." I found out later that little godly woman did know what she was talking about. Jim was drinking. He could hide it from the deacons and hide it from the preacher and hide it from the church and hide it from his own children but it is pretty hard for a man to hide his sins from his wife.

That little dying woman was saying look out Jim, you are not going to make it the way you are going. I'm terribly afraid Jim is not going to make it. She has been gone now for several years and as far as I know now Jim is still drinking, last time I heard. I'm afraid Jim will never make it to heaven. God says, no drunkard shall enter the kingdom of heaven. He is not going in where that little woman has gone I'm terribly afraid. Don't tell me she wasn't talking one moment to somebody on the other side then talking to us.

I had a man yonder in my community who was unsaved. He had a big heart but he had a terrible sin, drinking was his downfall.

When his sister died, I thought this was the time. I went over to see him and the man prayed and made promises to God. We put her away. No sooner had we buried her than right back to the liquor bottle. Then his mother died. That broke his heart. I can see him now literally crawling around on his living room floor promising God that he would give up his drink and that he would turn to Jesus and begin to live a holy and godly and spiritual life. That's a wonderful thing to say. But, he just didn't do it. No sooner had we buried her than right back to his drunkenness again. Then he had a cousin who was a very godly woman. She came to the end of life's journey about a year after his mother died. She went into a coma and everybody thought she was gone. All of a sudden, she brightened up and said you go call him. He walked into her presence and she looked into his face and said I've seen the face of Jesus. I've seen the face of your mother. I have seen the face of your sister and they tell me to tell you not to let the circle be broken. Within three months time that man was on his death bed calling for his liquor bottle and the name of Jesus in the same breath, almost the same breath as he died on that awful night. Don't tell me that there is not a heaven and that there is life beyond the grave! Through the lips of that dying cousin of His came the warning to him of his condition and urged him to come to the Lord Jesus Christ.

I have stood by too many death beds to doubt for a moment that there is a life beyond the grave. One time in Atlanta I went to my broadcast for about a month and urged friends to write in similar experiences of loved ones dying and I had a deluge of letters that came back to me telling of similar experiences that would hold up in any court room of law in the land as prime evidence of any truth. There is a land beyond without a shadow of a doubt!

Now the question that comes to us so many times, will we know each other there? I was preaching down in Charleston, South Carolina during the war days. I had gotten into the message one night and a little lady came to me in tears and she said, I want to ask you a question, will we know each other in heaven? I said, why do you ask? She said, Well I had a little girl 6 years of age, an only child and she died and she said, preacher I thought I couldn't stand it for a little while. She said I tuned in your broadcast one day and you said God doesn't make any mistakes when he takes our loved ones. That helped me a little bit. Then she looked at me and you could tell that mother's arms were hungry to press that little babe to her bosom again. She said, tell me, will I meet my little girl again. Will I be her mother? Will she be my child? Will we sustain that sweet relationship that we enjoyed in this world over there on the other side?

What do you think I said to her? What would you say to somebody if they asked you a question like that? Of course, you have to tell them what the Bible says. There came to mind the text presented to you at the outset of the message tonight, in fact that was the birth of this message. Jesus says, we are going to sit with Abraham and Isaac and Jacob in the kingdom of the heavens. Does that mean I will sit by Abraham and not know him and sit by Isaac and not know him and I'll sit by Jacob and not know him? I'll sit by my mother and not know her? I'll sit by my dad and not know him? I'll sit by my baby brother and not know him? I'll sit by my wife and not know her, my children and not know them?

Is heaven a place of ghosts? Is heaven a place where specters flit around in semi-darkness hither and yon or is heaven a place of glorious fellowship and light. One of the most comforting scriptures in the Bible for the child of God is that found in Colossians where God's Word says that we now have the inheritance saints in light. Light is a synonym for heaven and light means complete knowledge.

I say to you my friends I'll sit by Abraham and I'll know him. I'll sit by Isaac and I will know him. I'll sit by Jacob and I'll know him. I'll see Moody. I'll see Sunday. I'll see all the saints that have gone on and I'll see Isaiah and Mother and Dad and, we are going to know everybody and we won't need any introductions to them there. We will know them instantly. It is wonderful to know we are going to know our loved ones in heaven.

Now to be sure there won't be any babies there. There won't be any young men and young women. There won't be any male and female. God's Word says that in heaven we will be as the angels of God. Angels of God are sexless. Angels of God do not have degrees of age.

At the close of one of my meetings in South Carolina a lady told me that her husband died about a year ago, they had lived together some 40 years. You could tell she was broken hearted. She said, will I know my husband and will I be his wife over there? Well I had to tell her no she wouldn't be his wife in the sense because God's Word says they are neither married nor given in marriage but are as the angels of God, and are sons of God being sons of the resurrection. If you have a sense of loss in that, don't worry, you won't have any loss because over yonder in heaven it will be one big family and that relationship we enjoy down here in that sense of the family relationship will be among all the people of God in glory. We will be one big family. We will know each other and there will be abounding love and there will be no sense of loss whatsoever.

When I said there wouldn't be any babies there I didn't mean that babies wouldn't go to heaven. Please don't misunderstand me and go out of here and say that Brother Hendley said that babies do not go to heaven because I must tell you what I mean. I mean that heaven is a place of maturity and babyhood and youth is a time of immaturity and there will be no immaturity in heaven. There will be only maturity in heaven. When God created Adam and Eve He created them full grown and they weren't babies. They didn't go through youth and babyhood and infancy and all that sort of a thing but were full grown. We are going to have a full maturity in heaven with the Lord. We will be one big happy family in God. What a wonderful time it is going to be to be among our loved ones that have been born again!

All the questions are going to be answered over there. Now, all of them are not answered here. I am not going to stand up here and tell you that even the Bible answers all the questions. I have studied it 28 years and to this hour I don't understand why God let's this world rock on in its agony. That doesn't keep me from being a believer. I love God. I'm not bitter about it. I just don't understand it. There isn't any answer. There's no answer found in the Bible. I don't understand it. Someday God will make it plain to us over yonder but not here in this world. There are a lot of questions I don't know.

One of these days I want to sit down with the Lord and ask Him why He let my mother suffer like He did. I don't understand it. The first memory I have of my mother in that big two-story home, back in the bedroom was a large medicine cabinet filled with medicine bottles. Mother would go down stairs and fix a meal and then she would go drink her milk and take her medicine. She did that in all the years that I can remember. If anybody said, do this, she did it. Or do that, she did that. She went to the best doctors in Atlanta. Had the best medical attention. They treated her for some sort of a stomach ailment. But the autopsy proved that all that while she had cancer. It was an awful experience. I remember when we sent her off down to Florida hoping that might help her.

She came back home and I remember how shocked I was as a boy when I saw her terrible condition. She could scarcely get up the terminal steps in Atlanta. We took her to the hospital. I hadn't been married but about six months at that time. I was a lost church member. A lost preacher's son. I knew a lot about the Bible. I went to church regularly but I had not been born again. I didn't know Jesus in my heart. I went out there that night to see my mother. She was very bright, she had a cheerful, type personality. A wonderful personality. I thought maybe she was going to be alright. We went home and retired.

At twelve thirty my telephone rang. Mother was gone. The nurse had slipped out of the room and slipped back in and she had slipped out into eternity to be with God. I tell you right now friends, I buckled down to this old Bible and I began to search to find out where she went and I found Jesus as my Savior. I was sitting on my front porch reading the Word of God when the Lord Jesus came into my heart and gave me the new birth. Gave me the guarantee of heaven and heaven became real and the glory of the other world began to flood my soul. What a wonderful thing. One of these days when we get over yonder on the other side I want to ask Jesus why He let my mother suffer like she did. I don't understand it. I've never known any suffering like that. He'll tell me and I'll understand and I'll be satisfied. I don't know now but someday He'll make it plain.

I had a young couple yonder in my church 28 years of age. They didn't have any children. They prayed and said, Oh God, if you will give us a child we will give the child back to you. So God visited them and gave them a little baby girl. I never saw anybody so happy in my life. They dedicated it to the Lord. Maybe it will be missionary. We'll train it in a family altar. We'll read the Bible and pray with it and take it to church and Sunday School. Oh, what that couple promised they would do for that baby. After about three months God reached down and pulled it back into eternity in death. It broke their hearts. We took the little body down to Tucker, Georgia, to a little country church yard. I remember the little pitiful casket sitting on those little two by fours. I made my remarks and when I got through they began to lower that little casket with that little baby in its dead body in it into the earth. That woman began to cry and her husband reached over and pulled her into his arms and tried to kiss her tears away. Then they turned and looked at me the preacher and said, preacher, why did God take our baby? A lot of people don't want any children. We prayed for this child. A lot of people raise their children for the devil and hell. We had promised God we would raise our child for the Lord. Why did God take our child?

I couldn't tell them, All I could tell them is that in the coming years, it may be in that better land, we'll read the meaning of our tears and then sometime we'll understand. Until then, praise God faith sings, God knows the way. He holds the key. He guides us with unerring hand. Someday with tearless eyes we'll see Him there sometime and we'll understand. God is going to make it plain to us someday.

I can't tell you why some people die in infancy and some people get to old age. Why some people are sick all their lives and some robust in health. Some are born idiots. Some with super-intelligence. I can't tell you these things. I don't know. But I'll tell you one day over on the other side when we ask God He'll sit down and tell us and we'll be satisfied with the way He has been running this whole business.

There is a heaven. Jesus says they are coming from the east and the west all over the earth. Men and women, boys and girls, red and yellow, black, white who believe on Him and put faith in Him in spite of all the questions. They'll sit down with Abraham and Isaac and Jacob in the kingdom of heaven. But everybody is not going to heaven Jesus says. He says, the children of the kingdom shall be cast out in outer darkness and there shall be weeping and gnashing of teeth. Who are the children of the kingdom? They are the people who have the externals of religion but nothing of the internals of religion. They do not know Christ in their heart.

Some young man comes to the gate of heaven and raps on the gate and says, let me in and the angel says how do you expect to come in here? He says, my mother is in there. She prayed for me. Your mother prayed for herself. You mother lived a godly life. If your mother's prayers made a ladder to heaven you could never climb to heaven on those prayers. You must pray for yourself. That boy is shut out while his mother is shut in.

THE WORLD CRISIS AND THE ONLY WAY OUT

A godly mother one time who tried to lead her children to Christ and they wouldn't listen to her came down to the breakfast table one morning and told the story of a dream she had had that night. She said, I dreamed that the great judgment had taken place and Jesus was the Judge. I tried to tell you if you don't accept Him as Savior you will have to take Him as judge. All judgment is committed into the hands of the Son. The one that died for you will be the one who will sentence you to hell. He will say depart from me. She said, I saw Jesus sitting on the judgment seat, we were right in the midst of the great assembly. The Son of God said, bring the mother and the children. The mother goes to the right hand, she was the sheep. The children go to the left hand they are goats. You grabbed my skirts and began to weep. She said, I began to cry because I didn't want to be separated from you anymore than you wanted to be separated from me. Then an angel touched me and rendered me super natural and sublime and I raised myself and said, my children I tried to teach you the ways of God and you wouldn't walk in them. Now all I can say is Amen to your condemnation and you were led away to hell while I was led to heaven.

My beloved friends, that's no dream. That's taking place constantly. That's going to take place. There are families separated. Children from parents. parents from children. Unsaved from the saved, because they don't walk in the ways of God. The children of the kingdom Jesus said shall be cast down. Do you notice, Jesus says that nobody goes willingly to that lost world? You have to go. You will be cast out. You may not be concerned tonight about your soul my friends but I'll tell you unerringly you will be when that last breath leaves your body and that soul of yours takes the leap out of your body and an angel catches that soul of yours and holds you over that bottomless pit and you look down in that awful pit and you hear the moans and groans and the screams of torched men, women, boys and girls then you will quiver in your mind and you will crack and you would to God you had looked after the interests of your soul.

It is said the unsaved are cast into outer darkness. What does it mean preacher? I don't know. I never intend to know. I pray God that nobody in this room will ever experience what Jesus meant by being cast into outer darkness on the outside of heaven. One thing I do know it means hopelessness. Somebody has well said, on every link of the chain that binds an unsaved soul in hell are engraved with the words, forever and ever. That's the tragedy of it all. Then what is their condition? Jesus said, weeping and gnashing of teeth. Jesus says it.

I stood by a lady who was coming out from under an anesthetic from a very serious operation at Georgia Baptist hospital in Atlanta. She was groaning in her pain, oblivious to anybody being around. I said, this is Brother Hendley, I have come to pray with you. She turned her pitiful face toward me. She said, preacher, if hell is anything like what I am going through with, I don't want to go and I don't want anybody else to go. I tell you it is a place said Jesus, outside of heaven, of weeping and gnashing of teeth.

My friends, tonight there are two observations I want to make in conclusion as we have thought about heaven. The first is, that death is the doorway to heaven or hell for everyone us in this room. If I told you truthfully tonight that that door of your home where you enter it leads to hell you would try to avoid it as far as the east is from the west. If I told you truthfully that that door of your home opened upon a glorious heaven you wouldn't mind going through that door. There is a door you and I are going through inevitably if Jesus tarries, it is the doorway of death. On the other side you are going to find heaven or hell according to what you have done with the Lord Jesus Christ. Death, the Bible teaches is the doorway instantly to heaven or hell for every one of us under this tent. Men, women, boys and girls.

The second observation I want to make tonight from the Bible is that the Bible locates hell within the sight of heaven. You say what do you mean? I mean this. A lady came to me one night. She said, you have been talking about hell and you have been talking about heaven as the Bible does. I'm saved and I am going to be in heaven, how am I going to be happy in heaven when I know my husband is in hell? He died without Christ. I said, lady, you won't know you ever had that husband. You will forget him. You will never remember he ever existed. God will root the memory of him out of your mind.

A mother said, how can I be happy in heaven when my children are lost and in hell. You won't know they ever lived. You won't know that you ever had those children. God will root them out of your mind. People in heaven are not going to be disturbed by souls in hell. You say there is going to be a tremendous transformation, we are disturbed down here. Yes, and rightfully so and we had better try our dead level best to get them in out of the fire. What's the difference? The difference is that up there, God says the former things will not remembered in the new heavens and earth. The former things shall not be remembered nor come into mind. God is going to blot it out. Then again God says, He is going to wipe away all tears from our eyes and there will be no more sorrow or crying, or pain. There is not going to be any tears in heaven, not yonder in God's glorious heaven. He has promised to wipe away all our tears and that there will be no more sorrow. That means you can't suffer over some soul that is lost and in hell. You had better get your husband to Christ now. You had better get your wife to Christ now. You had better get your children to Jesus now because you will forget them through the ages of eternity in that lost world.

Will you listen to me? If you are unsaved sitting here tonight and you do not know you are saved, God's Word teaches the opposite for the unsaved. God's Word teaches that unsaved souls will see the saved in heaven. You will see your loved ones, your friends, those Christians you knew that talked to you and tried to get you to Jesus and prayed for you and you turned down their Christ and their entreating and their importunities. You will see them in heaven. That will make your hell two-fold more a hell. You want the scripture don't you and I want to be scriptural. God's Word says, there shall be weeping and gnashing of teeth when you see Abraham, Isaac, Jacob in the kingdom of heaven and you yourselves thrust out. You will see them but you will see yourself thrust out. Oh, what a hell it must be to see God's redeemed in glory and you can't get there, it must make hell two-fold more a hell. But it is the Word of God.

Now if what I preached to you tonight is true, and it is because it is the Bible and the Word of God, I want to say to you that the most foolish thing that a human being can do is to fail to make sure of heaven. I was sitting in my study one day and there came a phone call from a young lady weeping. She was from over in Sylvan Hills, close by where I live. She said, there was a terrible accident, preacher, will you come over and see Mother? She said my 28-year-old brother was killed. She choked up then she got a hold of her emotions and she said we can't calm Mother. We can't quiet her. She needs some help, will you come? I said, I'll come. I drove over. They ushered me into the room and there was this woman on this bed weeping her eyes out. Great agony. I read the scripture to her. I prayed with her. I reasoned with her. I did everything I knew to do to help her. I wasn't getting anywhere and I knew something was unusually wrong. So finally I said, woman, tell me, what is wrong. I said, nothing I say helps you. Nothing God says helps you. I have read the Bible. I have prayed. I have reasoned with you. I have given you everything I know that comforts other hearts in the time of death, when death comes and strikes at our door, tell me, why aren't you comforted?

She sat bolt upright in bed and looked me in the face and solemnly said, preacher, my son lived 28 years in this world and rejected Jesus Christ every day he lived and did not make certain about his soul, and now he is dead and he is in hell and I am going to heaven and I will never see him again. There is no comfort for me. She flung herself on that bed and resumed her weeping. 28 years God gave him in this life. 28 years with one thing paramount. What is it? To get ready for heaven. To miss hell and get ready for heaven. What does it matter about a job? What does it matter about automobiles? What does it matter about houses and wives and husbands and children and furniture and the 10 thousand and one things when a man hasn't looked after his soul? 28 years, 28 years. He is in hell. 28 years he heard the Gospel. 28 years he heard Jesus died for him. 28 years he heard the story of the cross. 28 years he had God's invitation to heaven ringing in his ears. 28 years he turned it down every time he heard it. Then an accident and he is in hell. He is lost. So many people get so close but never come.

Yonder, a famous vessel by the name of Royal Charger was approaching Liverpool England loaded with passengers. Just 24 days out the vessel caught fire and went down and everybody lost their lives. When the report came to the shore on Sunday morning, it came the duty of a godly preacher to go tell a little wife her husband would never come home. He raped on that cottage door at six o'clock in the morning. A little girl came skipping to the door, hello preacher, daddy will be here in a little bit come on in. She went skipping back to the kitchen and said, mommy here is the preacher. As soon as she could wipe her hands and get the biscuits off so she could see him for a minute, a breakfast she was preparing for a husband she would never see, she walked in to him and she started with a smile to say, preacher, my husband will be, then she said what's the trouble? The man of God said, madam, I bring you ill tidings. The vessel went down one day out from port and you husband was drowned in the depths of the sea. That poor little woman screamed as she fell to the floor in agony, O God, so near but he will never come! So near but he will never come. I thought about souls that get so near. So near to accepting Jesus. So near to heaven. So near to making sure but never quite do it and lose and miss for eternity. It is not enough to almost be a Christian. To be almost saved is to be altogether lost! Almost, but he will never come. Almost but that man will never come. That woman, that boy or that girl, almost.

Beloved, nothing matters but to make heaven. Nothing matters but to make sure of heaven. Make sure you are not going to hell and make sure you are going to heaven. That's all that matters. That's the big thing. Yonder in my church was a deacon who had 5 children. He lost 3 out of the 5 under humanly tragic circumstances. His little daughter Jimmie Lou when I was preaching one morning at twelve years of age walked down the isle and accepted Jesus. She joined the church. I had the privilege of baptizing her. Later when she fell in love with a young man there and they were to be married, I had the privilege of officiating at the wedding. God visited that union and gave them a little baby girl. One day Jimmie Lou was in the grocery store picking up groceries and over here her baby was in a buggy. A boy behind the counter was flipping a 38 revolver around his finger and she turned around and said, is that gun loaded? He said, yes mam. She said, please don't be flipping it around like that it might go off. She had no sooner turned her back than there was a terrible explosion. The bullet struck her in the back. It tore a big gapping hole in her stomach. With the blood flying she rushed toward the door. A neighbor who knew her saw her coming to that door in her condition and grabbed her and put her in the car and in seven minutes was five miles out from that place running just as fast as he could go. Got down to the hospital and that child was sitting in a pool of blood, when they marched down and picked her up and took her upstairs and put her to bed. They began to fight for her life. That precious girl, how those doctors and interns fought. I'll always admire those men. They were determined to save her life if they could.

They took the baby down there and they intensified their efforts. They were going to save that little mother to raise that child if medical science could do it. They got the best advice of the best doctors in the city. They stayed up day and night, they fought for her life but it was a losing battle. They dipped pints of pus out of her body. The afternoon when Jimmie Lou died she called for her mother to bring her baby and her mother brought the baby and leaned the little thing down to this little dying mother's lips and she planted a kiss on her baby's cheek and she said, Mamma, take care of my baby. The she

116

Precious Memories

"In October 1968, I was completing my education at New Orleans Baptist Theological Seminary when God led me to understand and admit that I had learned a great deal about God, but I did not know Him. During that time of deep conviction and soul searching, I gave up my whole life to the Lord.

Not long after that, I was blessed to be introduced to Evangelist Jesse Hendley. I had incurred quite a bit of criticism and questioning about the fact that I had been a pastor for ten years and was almost to the end of the ThD process at NOBTS and had not been born again.

I had been called to follow Adrian Rogers as pastor of First Baptist Merritt Island, Florida. The first person I called was Brother Jesse. He came and preached a revival for us. Many people came to the Lord. We had an old fashioned evangelistic revival meeting.

During his stay with us, he talked to me about the resistance he had experienced as he preached the Word of God without compromise. He identified with some of the challenges I had been facing. After a week with him and later two more weeks of revival at Whitesburg Baptist in Huntsville, Alabama, I was emboldened to preach God's Word, true and powerful, inspired and inerrant, no matter what others may say and do. The impact Brother Jesse had on my life, family, and ministry has been beyond my ability to describe. This humble, brilliant, courageous, loving man was my father in the ministry. I pray that his words will inspire and strengthen every person who has the privilege to read these great life changing messages from one of God's choicest servants."

Jimmy Jackson, Pastor Whitesburg Baptist Church

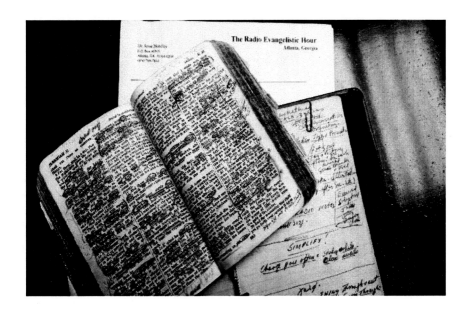

Brother Jesse's original Bible

THE WORLD CRISIS AND THE ONLY WAY OUT

sword: for the mouth of the Lord hath spoken it. And the destruction of the transgressors and of the sinners shall be together, and they that forsake the Lord shall be consumed.... Enter into the rock, and hide thee in the dust, for fear of the Lord, and for the glory of his majesty. The lofty looks of man shall be humbled, and the haughtiness of men shall be bowed down, and the Lord alone shall be exalted in that day. For the day of the Lord of hosts shall be upon every one that is proud and lofty, and upon every one that is lifted up; and he shall be brought low; ... And they shall go into the holes of the rocks, and into the caves of the earth, for fear of the Lord, and for the glory of his majesty, when he ariseth to shake terribly the earth. In that day a man shall cast his idols of silver and his idols of gold, which they made each one for himself to worship, to the moles and to the bats; To go into the clefts of the rocks and the tops of the ragged rocks, for fear of the lord, and for the glory of his majesty, when he ariseth to shake terribly the earth."

The Day of the Lord. A phrase that runs through the Old and the New testaments is coming upon a world that has forgotten God and shut Jesus Christ out of their individual lives. In Isaiah, the 63rd chapter we have the picture of Jesus returning in judgment upon an unbelieving world. A world that is largely unbelieving. For everybody that knows Isaiah 53 there are very, very few that knows Isaiah 63. In Isaiah 53, we have our Lord when He came the first time to die as a Savior for sinners, and to offer Himself as a Savior. In Isaiah 63, we have Him coming in judgment to trample His enemies beneath His feet. One of the most terrific promises in the Word of God. It isn't a converted world God's Word pictures for us but the very opposite when Jesus comes.

Here in the form of two questions the Prophet puts these words, "Who is this that cometh from Edom, with dyed garments from Bozrah? This that is glorious in his apparel, traveling in the greatness of his strength? (back came the answer of Christ) I that speak in righteousness, mighty to save." Then the second question. "Wherefore art thou red in thine apparel, and thy garments like him that treadeth in the wine fat? (Here is Jesus' terrible answer. It is hard to believe it) I have trodden the winepress alone; and of the people there was none with me; for I will tread them in mine anger, and trample them in my fury; and their blood shall be sprinkled upon my garments, and I will stain all my raiment. For the day of vengeance is in mine heart, and the year of my redeemed is come." There is the Lord Jesus coming back, not as the Savior but as the judge for everyone who had rejected Him as Savior and Lord. Back to a world that has refused Him, trampling His enemies beneath His feet. What a terrific moment.

Now, that we are face to face with that day of the Lord it is very evident from the Book of Joel. In Joel, the 3rd. chapter verse 9 is a passage that is being fulfilled before our eyes right now of prophecy. "Proclaim ye this among the Gentiles; Prepare war, wake up the mighty men, let all the men of war draw near; let the men come up: Beat your plowshares into swords, and your pruning hooks into spears: let the weak say, I am strong." I say to you that that passage is being fulfilled before our eyes. What is the great proclamation among the nations today? Prepare war. The greatest amount of money in America is going not to weapons of peace but weapons of destruction. That same thing is true around the world today. That is true with some 73 percent of our income going into weapons of mass destruction but it is true of England and it is true of Russia and it's true my friends of all the nations of the earth today.

The great proclamation is, prepare for war. We are living in the crisis of the world and Joel's prophecy is being fulfilled before our eyes. "Proclaim you this among the Gentiles, prepare war, wake up your mighty men, let all the men of war draw near; let them come up; Beat your plowshares into swords, and your pruning hooks into spears; let the weak say, I am strong." God's Word says, "Assemble yourselves, and come all ye nations, and gather yourselves together round about: ... Let the nations be wakened, and come up, to the valley of Jehoshaphat: for there will I sit to judge all the nations round about. Put ye in the sickle, for the harvest is ripe; come, get you down; for the press if full, the fats overflow; for their wickedness is great." Whose wickedness? The wickedness of the nations in the eyes of a holy God. "Multitudes, multitudes in the valley of decision; for the day of the Lord is near in the valley of decision. The sun and the moon shall be darkened, and the stars shall withdraw their shinning. The Lord also shall roar out of Zion, and utter his voice from Jerusalem and the heavens and the earth shall shake: but the Lord will be the hope of His people, and the strength of the children of Israel."

I can go on reading to you tonight from God's Word the fact that we are living in a world crisis and that we are approaching that terrible period of God's outpoured wrath upon a world rejecting His Son that is described in the Prophets and the Apostles as the day of the Lord. The day when God won't put up with human sin any longer. A human rebellion in human sin but will judge a world of sinners who have rejected Him. Now face to face in history and facing the day of God's wrath and judgment. What is our hope? The answer is, our only hope is in Jesus. Christ in you is your only hope of glory. It's the only hope for us nationally. It's our only hope individually. It's Christ in the individual heart, our only hope of glory.

Now the Lord Jesus Christ is the most wonderful being that this world has ever known. Back yonder 500 years before He was born God showed to the Prophet Isaiah the Lord Jesus as the great Savior, the Savior of the world. His great saving work. Isaiah cried out, "He is wonderful." I say to you my friends; Jesus Christ is the most wonderful being that the world has ever known. Jesus Christ is wonderful in His preincarnate glory and heavenly life for remember that Jesus was with God as the Son of God long before the human race ever came into being or God created the heavens and the earth. We read in the Book of John chapter 1, "In the beginning was the Word, and the Word was with God, and the Word was God. The same was in the beginning with God. All things were made by Him; and apart from Him was not anything made that was made."

There we have Jesus Christ, the Son of God, as the great creator. He is the one that made all the foul of the air. The fish of the sea. He is the one that created every creature, the sands of the seashore, this Jesus we talk about, the great creator, by Him were all things created in heaven and earth, doesn't make any difference what it is. He was wonderful in His preincarnate glory before He ever became a man yonder with His father in the great act of creation. Then Jesus Christ was wonderful with His virgin birth. He was born unlike any other person that has ever been born in this world. You and I were born in sin. We were born of our father, our parents, our fathers and mothers transmitted to us a sinful nature, a sinful disposition. But not Jesus Christ. Jesus Christ was born holily. Jesus Christ never knew sin. God's Word said He is "holy, harmless, undefiled, separate from sinners, and made higher than the heavens." When the holy ghost overshadowed the womb of the virgin Mary then God said, that holy thing, speaking of the body into which God stepped, shall be called the Son of God, I say to you, my friends, some people say it doesn't make any difference whether Jesus was virgin born or not. It makes the difference between heaven and hell. It makes the difference between salvation and damnation for believe me no sinner will ever be able to save a sinner. It takes a sinless being to save a sinner. I tell you Jesus Christ was sinless in His virgin birth.

Then Jesus Christ was wonderful in His miraculous life. He shook this world as nobody ever shook it. He has had the greatest influence on the human race that anyone has ever made. Jesus Christ was wonderful in His miraculous life.

He was wonderful in His teachings. Today, after some 28 years of studying this Bible, this Book, His words burn my soul like no other words I can read in all the libraries of this land. The words of Jesus. One time Daniel Webster said, I have read through the Sermon on the Mount, and when he got up he said, I say unto you I know man, it was more than man that spoke that word. I say to you it was more than man. His words have transformed the lives of tens of thousands of people. He was wonderful my friends in His teachings.

He is wonderful in His healings, He went about doing good, healing all that were oppressed of the devil. He was wonderful in His miracles. He proved He was God by the mighty works that He did. He stilled the tempest of the sea. He raised the dead. He cleansed the leper. He cast out demons. He proved Himself to be God by the miraculous works, the mighty works that only God could do. He was wonderful in His miracles. Jesus Christ was wonderful my friends, not only in His miracles but His power over the spirit world, even demons, going out of demons, possessed people cried out, we know thee who thou art, the holy one of God. The demon world knew Him to be the Son of God.

Then Jesus Christ was wonderful in His love for sinners. He did not repel men, He impelled them to come to Himself. His winsomeness, His forgiving spirit. His marvelous mercy. Jesus would pass by a thieving publican lining his pockets with the gold of others and say to him, Matthew, follow me, and that man forsakes a life of dishonesty and becomes Matthew a writer of a New Testament Book. Jesus Christ would pass by a fallen woman and she saw something in His face and His forgiveness that made her want to be pure and chaste and clean and holy and made her despise her sin. She became on the spot, transformed and followed Him, a changed being. Jesus was wonderful in His miraculous life.

Then Jesus was wonderful in His atoning death as He died for sinners. As He died for you. As He died for me. It was my privilege in July one year ago to be in Notre Dame cathedral in Paris France. When I stood there surveying the cathedral I remembered reading that years ago there was a man preaching there in that cathedral and he told this story. He said, some years ago there came into this cathedral three profligate youths from wealthy families. One of them made a bet with another and said, you won't go over there to the priest and make a bogus confession. This young man took up his bet, being very venturesome, so he said, I will. He started over to the priest and made a bogus confession. The old priest, being pretty wise in the ways of man read what was in the young man's heart, so he said to the young man as he began to make his confession of sin, he said, Son, if you mean what you are saying I want you to go over there to the foot of that crucifix and look up in the bleeding face of the Son of God and say, Jesus, all this you did for me and I don't care.

When he realized the old priest was calling his hand, he wasn't going to be backed down so he swaggered over to do that. As he knelt and looked up into the bleeding face of the Son of God he bowed his head as he started to say Jesus, all this you did for me, then he broke off and dropped his head into his hands and began to sob for it dawned on him for the first time in his life the Son of God died for me. Jesus died for me. It broke his heart. With his eyes streaming with tears he rushed out of that great building a transformed man. When that man told the story, he paused and dramatically said, I that speak unto you was that young man. His life was transformed when he looked up into the bleeding face of Jesus and he couldn't say Lord, you did this for me but I don't care.

I say to you my friends, there isn't a man or woman or boy or girl here who can look in the face of Jesus dying on the cross for your sins, and you can't get up off your knees and walk away and say Jesus, you died for me and I don't care. I do care, Lord. I do care enough to trust you as my Savior. Enough to give you my life. Enough to give you the rest of my days. I do trust you Lord. He is wonderful in His atoning death. Christ died for your sins. That's the heart of the Gospel. Christ died for our sins according to the Scriptures and He did it individually. You will not have to pay for your sins if you receive Him as your Savior and Lord He is wonderful in His atoning death.

Then Jesus Christ was wonderful, praise be to His Name in His glorious resurrection. The greatest fact I know tonight after the death of Jesus is He is alive today. Jesus is alive right now. Right this very moment. You say Brother Hendley, how do you know Jesus Christ is alive? I know for several reasons. First reason I know Jesus is alive is I believe the testimony of these men who said that they ate and drank and slept with Him and touched Him and handled Him for 40 days and 40 nights after His resurrection from the dead.

The only way I can believe in any personality of history beyond my own contact and my own generation is through credible witnesses who heard and saw them. I don't know that George Washington ever lived but I have to believe on the testimonies who lived in his day. I never saw George Washington. As far as I'm concerned and as far as my own personal knowledge is concerned he may have never existed. The only way I know Abe Lincoln ever lived were through credible witnesses who lived in his day.

The only way I can know about Jesus Christ is credible historians and witnesses. Listen to me friends, I've done a little reading in my days, these years. I have spent most of my life reading books. The Bible and other books. And I am saying to you if there is any personality in history that I can believe in its in Jesus Christ. If there are any historians that I do believe, if there are any human beings upon whose word I can depend, it is the word of these holy, godly men who at the jeopardy of their lives wrote that they ate and drank and slept with Him 40 days and 40 nights after His resurrection from the dead. I believe Matthew wrote the truth. I believe that Mark wrote the truth. I believe Paul told the truth. I believe that Luke told the truth. If I can believe any historian I believe the sacred men who jeopardized their lives and most of them died in giving their witness to the fact of the resurrection of Jesus Christ. I believe those men if I believe any event in history.

But I have a better reason than that. You ask me why I know He lives. He lives within my heart. I could sooner doubt my life than I could doubt that fact. There are a lot of things I don't know. There is one thing I know tonight if I know anything. If I have any consciousness of knowledge, there is one thing I know. That is, when I was 20 years of age my precious mother slipped into eternity and I, a poor lost church member who had never met Jesus, never been born again, been around preaching all my life, my dad a minister, brought up in church, reading gospel books, but no Christ in my heart. No reality at all, just the externals of religion and no Jesus in my heart.

My precious mother died and I was shocked like never before. I wanted to know where she went. I wanted to follow her. I wanted to meet her again. I got this precious old book and began to read. Yonder, sitting on my front porch one day I read about Jesus as I had never read about Jesus before in my life and I opened my heart to Him. He stepped across the threshold of my heart that day and transformed my life. My life has been different these 28 years since I met Him. I can bear witness tonight as God is my witness, and I say it as reverently as I know Jesus Christ is as real to me as my mother was. Jesus is as real to me as my precious wife and my precious daughter and my precious son. Jesus Christ lives within my heart. I know that.

I remember yonder at Easter time some years ago when I was at Colonial Hills church, I was on the radio, I had to prepare a radio message each day so I stayed praying, these radio preachers know what I am talking about. I had to prepare my Sunday morning service Sunday morning, and Sunday evening on Sunday afternoon. There I was approaching the deadline, getting time for me to go down to the awaiting people at the church and no message. It was Easter Sunday morning. There I was pacing back and forth on the floor of my study praying for God to give me a message. All of a sudden God opened the windows of heaven and the glory of Jesus flooded my heart.

The risen, living Christ flooded that room and I rushed out of the consciousness of His presence through to my living room where my wife was sitting looking over her lesson and I was clapping my hands. She looked at me and said, what in the world is wrong with you? I said, honey, He appeared to me also just like He did the Apostle Paul. Paul said he was one born out of due time. Jesus has appeared to me also. He is real to me. Jesus Christ promises to manifest Himself to that heart that will open its door to Him. If any man loves me he will keep my word and I will come in unto him and manifest myself unto him. I'll make myself real to him if he will only open his heart's door to me. Jesus Christ is wonderful in His glorious resurrection. He is the living Savior and nothing but a living Savior will save your soul from your sins and from a devil's hell and can bring you to heaven. Nothing but a living Jesus.

When Charles Haddon Spurgeon, one of the greatest saints of God who has ever lived and knew Jesus; like so few men have ever known Jesus, because he paid the price, when he was dying, his little invalid wife bent over him as the old man of God was whispering and what do you think he was saying as he was dying? He said, wifey, I've had such a good time with my Lord Jesus, I have had such a good time with Jesus. The world thinks it is having a good time. The sinner thinks he is having a good time and he doesn't know what a good time is. A man that walks with Jesus Christ is the only man that knows what a good time is. What a good life is. I love that song, "And He walks with me and He talks with me and He tells me I am His own. The joys we share as we tarry there, none other has ever known." Jesus is alive, the risen, living Christ manifesting Himself to hearts that will open their doors to Him.

You friends tonight that really know Him know that I am speaking the truth. Some of you in this room would say, know Jesus? Do I know my wife? Do I know my son and daughter? I walk with Him. Of course I know Jesus! You know, just because you know, you do know because you walk with Him. But I want to say to others tonight, do you know Jesus? You would have to say, I know about Him. I've heard a lot about Him but I can't say that I am an intimate acquaintance with Jesus. I can't say He lives in my heart. I can't say that Christ in me is my hope of glory. Yet my friends that's your only hope. You have no hope of heaven unless Jesus is in your heart.

Now along with that truth about the Lord Jesus Christ I want to say a word to the Christians who are here tonight. That is this word. Christian, what are you doing with your life in the light of His great sacrifice for you? What are you doing with your life. What are you doing for Jesus who gave His blood and life for You? What are you doing for Him?

I was preaching in a southern city and a godly preacher's wife who knows something of the agonizing of a preacher, she said to me one night when I walked off the platform, she said, do you know you are killing yourself? I said to her, lady do you know what Paul said? He said, except a grain of wheat fall in the earth and die it abides alone, but if it die it will bring forth much fruit. You know the trouble, friends, we are not willing to die for the Lord and we can't live without death. Life comes out of death. Dying to self. Dying to the world. Dying to the flesh to live only for God. That's the only way that we can bear fruit for heaven.

There was this godly missionary out yonder who knew the secret of utter sacrifice to Jesus Christ to bear Fruit who wrote a little poem that I love very much.

Where are you ripened fields behold,
Waving to God their sheaves of gold,
Be sure some grain of wheat has died
Some saintly soul been crucified
Someone has wept and prayed,
And thought hell's legions undismayed.

We are going to reveal when we get to heaven that the great harvest in the spiritual field has been brought about as Christians have died to self and the flesh and the world and lived utterly for God, sacrificed everything for the Lord. We read concerning Jesus Christ the law of sacrifice, He said the zeal of God's house hath eaten me up. Zeal for God destroyed me physically. When they arrested Him they said you are not yet 50 years of age and you look 50 now when he was only about 30. Did the ravages of his labor for God and the cause of God and his utter sacrifice make him prematurely an old man when he was only 30 years of age?

It is written of John the Baptist that he was a burning and a shining light and that's in proper order. You are not going to do any shining if you are not willing to burn. You are not going to do it.

Paul the Apostle said the great passion of his life after he met Jesus was to know Him in the power of His resurrection, in the fellowship of His suffering being made conformable to His death, Paul said I want to die the death that Jesus died. What kind of a death did He die? A vicarious death. He died for others. Paul said, I want to follow the Lord. I want to give my life for others. I tell you friends, when we catch a glimpse of the Son of God's sacrifice for us we can never be the same.

Jesus said, if any man will come after me let him deny himself and take up his cross daily and follow me. No man can walk with me until he hates mother, father sister, brother, houses or lands. Seek ye first the kingdom of God and His righteousness and all these things shall be added unto you. Not second or third or fourth or tenth or twenty fifth but Jesus and His cause and souls come first when you are fully surrendered to the Son of God. When you realized what He has done for you. I want to ask you tonight, have you ever sacrificed, have you ever surrendered everything to Jesus? You will never know Him in all His glory like He can be to you until you surrender everything to the Lord Jesus.

I remember back yonder when Christ called me to preach. I remember that night that I fought that battle. I didn't want to. I was afraid very frankly. It isn't very pleasant when you see other lives planning to make a living in this world to utterly cast yourself entirely upon the Lord. If you think that life of utter faith is easy just try it sometime my friends. It isn't easy. I remember that night I had to fight the battle. In the early morning hours I said alright Lord, I'll be a preacher if you want me to be. I'll go where you want me to go and be what you want me to be. He called me into the ministry.

I preached for 14 years in one church. God blessed our ministry, blessed be His Name.

Then He called me to be an Evangelist, I remember that battle. It was the hardest battle I think I ever fought. Yonder in a hotel room, the Admiral Sims hotel in Mobile Alabama one Sunday afternoon. I was there in a revival. God was pressing me about the evangelistic field. There I had my church, 23 hundred members. I had my radio program. I had plenty of work to do. It wasn't a matter of work, it was a matter of the evangelistic fields white to harvest.

I went in that hotel room that afternoon greatly burdened. I locked myself in and got on my knees and the Lord Jesus paid me a visit. As He bent over me He said, I want your church. I said, Lord you can't have it. I have been here these 14 years and we have seen it grow to 23 hundred members and most of them my own converts, I love these people Lord, I can't leave it. He said, it is not your church son, it's mine. I said, alright Lord you can have it. I gave up that church. I haven't been back to this moment.

Then He said, I want your radio program. I said, Lord you can't have that radio program. I'm ministering to people here in the city. I'd like to keep it. I would like to be able to preach the Word every day over radio and to win souls. People write me of how they find Christ. Backsliders come back to God. The bereaved are comforted and weakened Christians are strengthened. The tempted are made courageous and souls are saved Lord, I'd like to keep the radio. He said, it isn't yours. It's mine. I gave it to Him. He took it away from me a year then He gave my radio broadcast back to me. We have stayed on now.

Then He asked me for the hardest thing He ever asked me, He said, I want your family. I want you to be away from your wife and your children most of the time. I want you to see your children grow up without a daddy. I want you to live the lonely life of an evangelist. That's the hardest thing Jesus Christ ever asked me to do. It wasn't easy then and it isn't easy now. I tried to get my wife by telephone but she was away, somehow I couldn't. I was just lonely in that hotel room. It isn't easy for me and it never will be. But I said, Lord, if you want my family, you can have everything I have. I'm willing to go anywhere you want me to go and be anything you want me to be.

I tell you friends, I wouldn't be back where I was for all the gold in the world. I'm saying to you tonight if there is a drop of blood in these veins that does not belong to the Son of God I pray God will lay me flat out right now. I don't want it.

I'll tell you what Jesus is looking for. A bunch of Christians who appreciate what He did when He gave His life and His all. Who will come at the foot of His cross and give up everything and seek His kingdom and His righteousness first and put Jesus and the love of God and love for one another and love for a lost world above all selfish interests. The Lord is looking for fully surrendered Christians. The least we can do is say, Jesus you died for me and I want to give my life to you. That is what the Lord is looking for.

May I repeat again Christian friend, you will never know Him like He wants you to know Him. You will never know Him like you can know Him. You will never know power, you will never know blessing. You will never know the reality of the Christ until your all is on the altar and you make the full surrender to the Lord Jesus Christ and put Him and His things first in your life. So much for the Christian. Christian, what will you do with your life in the light of His great sacrifice for you.

Then my final words tonight are to those who cannot say that Christ lives in me, my hope of glory. You who are unsaved, I'm asking you, what will you do with this great salvation tonight. Now before you answer me boys and girls, young men and young women, ladies and gentlemen, before you answer that question may I remind you if you do the wrong thing with Jesus it means eternal death. But if you do the right thing with Jesus it means eternal life. First of all, if you do the wrong thing with Jesus it means eternal death. If you reject Jesus Christ your soul shall be lost forever. It means eternal death.

Yonder in Atlanta a lady called me and asked me to go down to Grady hospital and see an orphan girl 18 years of age who was dying. I went down to see her. I visited her Thursday, Friday, and Saturday. Each time I begged that girl to accept Jesus. I talked to her as earnestly as I have ever talked to a soul. Each time she refused Christ. I would bow my head and have prayer for her then I would leave. On Saturday afternoon as I made my third call I said I am going to have to go now and I can't come back tomorrow. I have to be about my pulpit ministrations but the Lord willing I will try to come back Monday.

I went back Monday and the bed was empty. I said to a lady there in the ward, what happened to the little girl? I was shocked when she told me she had died Saturday night. I said to her with that agony in my heart, did she ever accept Jesus? She looked at me and she said, preacher we didn't the heart to tell you but every time that you would pray for that girl, close your eyes and pray for her after you had begged her to accept Jesus and she refused the Lord and you would close your eyes and be praying for her she would look at us and she would laugh and she would smirk and she would make fun of you as you were praying for her soul to be saved. I thought, poor little girl yonder in the flames of an awful devil's hell. You are not laughing and smirking and making fun of a man of God who honestly loved your soul and tried to get you to accept Jesus, no you are wishing before God that you had listened to this poor preacher and that you had yielded to the Son of God who alone could have saved you. But now there you are in a devil's hell forever.

Oh, beloved, if you do the wrong thing with Jesus. If you reject Him, it's eternal death. But listen, if you do the right thing with Jesus which is to receive Him into your heart as your Savior and Lord it will mean eternal life.

Yonder in Birmingham, Alabama I was preaching one day. A young boy, 17 years of age came among the others who came to Jesus that evening, the closing service of the campaign. I went on my way. Three weeks later I was in Louisiana when a telegram came from this preacher back in Birmingham, the 17-year-old boy who was saved in your meeting the other day and came to Christ was killed in a terrible accident just today. Wasn't it a glorious thing preacher that he got in just it time? When I was preaching that night to that young man trying to make him realize the urgency of the matter of accepting Christ, he might have said, oh, preacher what's the hurry, I'11 live to be 50. I'll live to be 25, he didn't. I'll live to be 20, he didn't. I'll live a month, he didn't. He was dead in three weeks. You know that night when I was preaching neither did I know, that he would be called into eternity in less than three weeks time. How glad that boy is that, that night as this poor preacher held before him Jesus he let Christ come into his heart. For Christ in him is his only hope of glory.

Let every head be bowed and every eye closed.

Precious Memories

"I had the privilege of hearing Jess Hendley preach only once in my life at Byne Memorial Church in Albany, GA, going there at the urging of my brother Jack for whom I had prayed for ten years before he was gloriously saved. After salvation, Jack had become a loyal follower of Jess Hendley at revival meetings around Atlanta, and on his radio broadcasts. After hearing Jess Hendley preach at Byne that night, I could understand why my brother had fallen in love with Jess's powerful preaching. Since my brother was later killed in accident every time I hear the name of Jess Hendley, the thought of Jack and Jess being together in heaven comes to my mind. I have prayed that every time a message from this book is read, another heart is touched for Jesus; Jack and Dr. Jess will be rejoicing together."

Bill Prince
Executive Minister
Biblical Principles Inc

THE WORLD CRISIS AND THE ONLY WAY OUT

Precious Memories

"Brother Jess was a dear friend to the Waters family for many years. Some of my earliest memories were being in revivals with my daddy, Macky Waters, when Brother Jess was preaching. One that stands out to me was Jess preaching at Colonial Hills in East Point, Georgia, a church he pastored for fourteen years, and many souls were saved. Our families' relationship goes back to the days before the depression. He and my grandfather, Clyde Waters, worked together at the Ford Motor Company on Ponce de Leon Avenue in Atlanta, where they built Ford Model T's together. From there, the two men would go on to impact their world for Christ, while remaining good friends along the gospel way. The relationship would grow even deeper through my uncle, Jimmy Waters. He preached many revivals for him at Mabel White Baptist Church in Macon. Only eternity could count the amount of souls saved in those meetings. He was a special man to me as well. I had the privilege to sit and learn at his feet in 1992; he told me this, "Love Jesus, love the Bible, and love souls, and the priority to warn them of their eternal destiny." Three generations of our family have been deeply influenced by the ministry of this Man of God. Though he be dead, yet he speaks."

Brad Waters
Pastor of First Baptist Church in Hazlehurst, GA

Audit Trail Statement for Permissions to Publish

The materials from which this book is prepared were transcribed from the actual audio tapes of the voice of Dr. Jesse Hendley recorded as he preached the sermons contained herein at Flint Michigan. We have attempted to print the exact words spoken by Dr. Hendley.

The personal effects of Dr. Jesse Hendley in part were kept by Pastor Danny Watters of the Beulah Baptist Church in Douglasville, Georgia in archives at the church.

Following the death of Dr. Jesse Hendley, Pastor Watters made attempts to place the materials into the possession of family members and others who might be interested in the memorabilia. The archived materials included hundreds of audio cassettes, many documents relating to the radio programs prepared by Dr. Hendley and, the actual radio equipment and microphone that Dr. Hendley used in his many radio broadcasts.

Pastor Danny Watters was unable to place the materials into the possession of anyone else despite his diligent search and contacts with the family. Therefore, he maintained the archives at the church even after he ceased to be the pastor at Beulah. Pastor Watters spent his last years as the Director of Pastoral Ministries at what was then called the Georgia Baptist Convention. When Pastor Watters became ill with a disease that eventually caused his demise, he began to make arrangements. One of the arrangements he made was for all of Dr. Jesse Hendley's archives to be transferred to the ownership of Pastor Brad Waters of the First Baptist Church of Hazlehurst, Georgia. Pastor Watters' Widow and Executor, made the transfer of ownership official during 2015.

During 2015 and 2016, a partnership was formed between Pastor Brad Waters and Bill Prince, Executive Minister of Biblical Principles Inc, a non-profit religious organization, who shared Pastor Brad Waters' vision to publish some of the works of Dr. Jesse Hendley. The purpose of this effort was to make Dr. Hendley's sermons available in the form of books which could be distributed at no charge to young pastors across America.

Working in concert, Bill Prince and Pastor Waters searched diligently for relatives of Dr. Hendley in order to obtain permission for publishing these works. When no living relatives or heirs could be contacted it was decided that the materials are public domain under the ownership and watch care of Pastor Brad Waters. It is under the authority of this statement of ownership and watch care that this material is published by Biblical Principles Inc.

Free Books for Ministers

As a memorial to Danny Watters a copy of this book may be provided free for ministers by Biblical Principles Inc. through the contact us form on www. biblicalprinciplesinc.org or by other means of distribution. Donations on line can be made on this website. All revenue from this book through royalties and donations are used to make free books for ministers possible.

Reader friend, here's one last thing. Do you know for sure that if you were to die today that you would go to heaven? If not and you need to settle your answer once and for all as "yes", please pray the following prayer then record and date your decision.

Oh God, in Jesus name I confess that I am a sinner and believing that Jesus died for me at Calvary and was resurrected, I repent, and place my trust in Jesus for Salvation.

Name _____

Date _____

CPSIA information can be obtained
at www.ICGtesting.com
Printed in the USA
FFOW05n2354051217

9 781945 698385